99 LIFE-GIVING BIBLE VERSES FOR WOMEN

WHEN WE ASK, GOD ANSWERS

HOPE JOHNSON

WHITAKER HOUSE

99 Life-Giving Bible Verses for Women
When We Ask, God Answers

hopeunyielding.com

ISBN: 979-8-88769-457-3
eBook ISBN: 979-8-88769-458-0

Printed in the United States of America

Whitaker House
1030 Hunt Valley Circle
New Kensington, PA 15068
www.whitakerhouse.com

Library of Congress Cataloging-in-Publication Data
Names: Johnson, Hope, 1991- author.
Title: 99 life-giving Bible verses for women : when we ask, God answers / Hope Johnson.
Other titles: Ninety-nine life-giving Bible verses for women
Description: New Kensington, PA : Whitaker House, [2025] | Summary: "Looks at characters throughout the Bible who faced pain, weariness, disillusionment, and discouragement yet ultimately discovered the goodness of God, suggesting Scriptures still address life situations today, with particular emphasis on women's issues"— Provided by publisher.
Identifiers: LCCN 2025008556 (print) | LCCN 2025008557 (ebook) | ISBN 9798887694573 (trade paperback) | ISBN 9798887694580 (ebook)
Subjects: LCSH: Christian women—Religious life. | Bible—Quotations.
Classification: LCC BV4527 .J6345 2025 (print) | LCC BV4527 (ebook) | DDC 248.8/43—dc23/eng/20250313
LC record available at https://lccn.loc.gov/2025008556
LC ebook record available at https://lccn.loc.gov/2025008557

1 2 3 4 5 6 7 8 9 10 11 ꟺ 32 31 30 29 28 27 26 25

CONTENTS

1: WHEN YOU FEEL UNSEEN

So Hagar gave this name to the L*ORD* *who had spoken to her: "You are the God who sees me," for she said, "Here I have seen the One who sees me!"*
—Genesis 16:13

"Does God truly see me?" It's a question that has haunted many of us in times of doubt. In a world with billions of people, the thought that the God of the universe sees you may seem too good to be true. But Hagar's story answers this question that lies heavy on our hearts with a resounding *yes*. God sees you, God knows you, and God loves you.

Hagar likely felt unseen. An Egyptian maidservant in the home of Abram and Sarai, she was treated less like a woman with thoughts and feelings and more like a means to an end. After years of barrenness, Sarai asked Abram to sleep with Hagar so that she could build a family through her, a common practice at the time. When Hagar conceived, however, enmity erupted between the women, and instead of rejoicing, Sarai treated her servant poorly. Abram didn't do much better, telling Sarai to do whatever she wanted with the mother of his unborn child. Worn down by the constant mistreatment, Hagar fled to the desert.

Imagine Hagar's shock and awe when the angel of the Lord found her in the wilderness and called her by name, saying, *"Hagar, servant of Sarai … where have you come from, and where are you going?"* (Genesis 16:8). The angel of the Lord gave her specific instructions: Return to Sarai and name her son Ishmael, encouraging her with the promise that her descendants would be *"too numerous to count"* (Genesis 16:10). In Hagar's awe, she became the first person in Scripture to give God a name, calling Him *"the God who sees me."* Abram didn't see Hagar. Sarai didn't see Hagar. But God saw Hagar—and He sees you too.

If you are questioning whether God sees you, reflect on Hagar's encounter with the angel of the Lord. The same God who pursued Hagar in the desert sees you, loves you, and will be with you, whatever comes.

Pray: *Father, You are the God who sees me. You know my name and my future, and You have sought me out and pursued a relationship with me. When I doubt, open my eyes to the ways that You have been pursuing me, loving me, and guiding my steps.*

2: WHEN YOU'RE GIVING GOD ADVICE

And Abraham said to God, "O that Ishmael might live under Your blessing!" But God replied, "Your wife Sarah will indeed bear you a son, and you are to name him Isaac. I will establish My covenant with him as an everlasting covenant for his descendants after him." —Genesis 17:18–19

When God told Abraham his wife would have a son, he laughed. It wasn't the first time the Lord had given this promise, but at their age, all hope was lost. Plus, they'd been down this road before with nothing to show for it. Nothing except Ishmael, of course, his child with Sarah's maidservant Hagar. Perhaps too tired to start hoping again, Abraham made a logical suggestion to God that would be easier on everyone: *"O that Ishmael might live under your blessing!"*

Like Abraham, many of us give God advice based on our understanding of the situation and our doubt that He can do the miraculous. We make a case for why God should do things our way, citing Scripture to support our points. But behind our flowery words and Scripture citations isn't a heart submitted to God, but one scrambling in fear that unless we carefully craft an argument for our heart's desires, He's going to forget about us.

Although, like Abraham, we might be saying "Lord," we are stripping Him of the title and claiming it as our own. We are really saying:

- "Lord, I know better than You; why can't You get with the program?"
- "Lord, if only my plan might live under Your blessing."

It's audacious to give advice to the Creator of the universe, but just as He was patient with Abraham, He is patient with us. God didn't condemn Abraham for his faithlessness but firmly repeated His promise of a son, a promise that came to pass within the year.

The next time you start giving God advice, remember the miraculous birth of Isaac that happened on God's terms, not Abraham's. Wait for His provision and trust that His plan for you is far better than any you could dream up.

Pray: *Lord, like Abraham, I've thought I know better than You. Many times, I have made a case for what I want and dug my heels in, demanding that You take my advice. In this moment, I surrender my idea of what is best, knowing that You are perfectly wise, good, and powerful. Help me to trust in Your wisdom when Your plan is different than mine.*

3: WHEN GOD FULFILLS A PROMISE

Now the LORD attended to Sarah as He had said, and the LORD did for Sarah what He had promised. So Sarah conceived and bore a son to Abraham in his old age, at the very time God had promised.
—Genesis 21:1–2

If any passage in Scripture says, "I told you so," it's this one. God's promise to Sarah and Abraham was impossible, so impossible, in fact, that both wife and husband laughed when they heard it. Abraham had even tried to convince God to do something a little more realistic—give the blessing to Ishmael, his son through Sarah's maidservant Hagar. But God wouldn't concede to Abraham and Sarah's disbelief and give them a different story than the one He had planned.

In these verses, we see an unchanging truth: *God does what He says He will do.* We hear this holy "I told you so" three times: "*Now the LORD attended to Sarah* ***as He had said****, and the LORD did for Sarah what* ***He had promised****. So Sarah conceived and bore a son to Abraham in his old age, at the very time* ***God had promised****.*" Despite Sarah's questioning and unbelief, God showed grace to her and did exactly what He said He would do.

Like Sarah, you may be struggling to believe one of God's promises. You may also feel that His Word is too good to be true. Scripture is bursting with promises that God will provide, that He will bring good out of suffering, and that He will be with us in our most difficult times, but in a dark world where opposing voices are loud, the fulfillment of these promises may seem as likely as getting pregnant at age ninety. But Scripture is also bursting with account after account of how God fulfilled His promises to people just like us. When you are doubting His promises, read the stories of the women and men in the Bible who saw God do what He said He would do. You can trust that you too will someday see, understand, and rejoice in that holy "I told you so" as you look back and see how God fulfilled His promises at just the right time and in just the right way.

Pray: *Father, I'm struggling to believe You will fulfill your promises, but I know that You always tell the truth and You always do what You say you do. When I struggle to believe, fill me with faith. You are the God of the impossible, whose Word never fails.*

4: WHEN GOD SURPRISES YOU

Then Sarah said, "God has made me laugh, and everyone who hears of this will laugh with me." She added, "Who would have told Abraham that Sarah would nurse children? Yet I have borne him a son in his old age."
—Genesis 21:6–7

Do you believe God wants to surprise you with good things? Many Christians assume that the route paved with the most suffering is the godliest one by default. While it's true that the Christian life is not easy—following Jesus requires swimming upstream against the culture and dying to yourself daily—our God is a good Father who gives good gifts to His children. (See Matthew 7:11.) Just as a good earthly father may surprise his daughter with a gift "just because," so is the abundance of God's gifts toward us. His gifts come in many forms, but a common thread is that they produce a godly joy and a sense of awe at His provision.

God's gift of Isaac to Sarah is a wonderful example of God surprising us with joy. Although Sarah had been promised she would bear a child in her old age, because of her doubt, she was *still* surprised when it happened. We are often the same, not expecting good things from God though He has promised that He is a good Father who gives good gifts.

Your Father in heaven is not looking at you sternly with His arms crossed, telling you to try harder, make yourself suffer, learn to enjoy pain. He sent His Son to walk the same dusty, broken ground that you do and understands your longings, weaknesses, hopes, and needs. He walks with you through the difficult times and refreshes you with good things.

As you look back on your life so far, can you think of any gifts, large and small, He has surprised you with? A striking sunrise? A word of encouragement? A new friend? Reflect on those good surprises from God and let them fill you with expectancy that He is indeed a good, personal Father who knows you intimately, loves you personally, and will surprise you with gifts of joy when you least expect it.

Pray: *Father, transform my mind so that I can see You as the good Father You truly are. Like Sarah, I often doubt that You want to bring good things into my life. Surprise me with gifts of Your goodness and give me eyes to see the gifts You put in my path.*

5: WHEN LOVED ONES DISAPPOINT YOU

Early in the morning, Abraham got up, took bread and a skin of water, put them on Hagar's shoulders, and sent her away with the boy. She left and wandered in the Wilderness of Beersheba. When the water in the skin was gone, she left the boy under one of the bushes. Then she went off and sat down nearby, about a bowshot away, for she said, "I cannot bear to watch the boy die!" And as she sat nearby, she lifted up her voice and wept. Then God heard the voice of the boy, and the angel of God called to Hagar from heaven, "What is wrong, Hagar? Do not be afraid, for God has heard the voice of the boy where he lies. Get up, lift up the boy, and take him by the hand, for I will make him into a great nation." Then God opened her eyes, and she saw a well of water. So she went and filled the skin with water and gave the boy a drink. —Genesis 21:14–19

Have you ever been let down by your loved ones when you needed them the most? Whether it was emotional support, a financial concern, or simply being there at an important time, they weren't able to give you what you needed.

Hagar, Sarah and Abraham's maidservant, was in a similar position. Once Sarah gave birth to Isaac, she wanted to send Hagar and her son Ishmael away to make sure Isaac would receive the inheritance. Though distressed, Abraham followed Sarah's lead and sent them into the desert. He provided them with a skin of water—temporary refreshment that soon ran out, leaving them to die. After the water ran out, however, *God brought Hagar and Ishmael to a well*, and they were saved.

Abraham did the best he could given the circumstances, but a mere skin of water was far from enough. The same applies to even the best of human relationships. They can offer us refreshment along our journey, but when we are at our weakest, dying of thirst, we cannot rely on the meager offerings of others. Even the best of friends, family, and spouses can't quench the deepest thirst inside of us. God often uses people to meet our needs, but Jesus is the living water who fully, eternally quenches our thirst. (See John 4:10–14.)

Pray: *Lord, please help me to give grace to my loved ones when they don't meet all my needs. You are the living water who quenches my deepest thirst. Open my eyes to the abundance of Your love and provision.*

6: WHEN GOD SAYS NO

When the LORD saw that Leah was unloved, He opened her womb; but Rachel was barren. And Leah conceived and gave birth to a son, and she named him Reuben, for she said, "The LORD has seen my affliction. Surely my husband will love me now." Again she conceived and gave birth to a son, and she said, "Because the LORD has heard that I am unloved, He has given me this son as well." So she named him Simeon. Once again Leah conceived and gave birth to a son, and she said, "Now at last my husband will become attached to me, because I have borne him three sons." So he was named Levi. And once more she conceived and gave birth to a son and said, "This time I will praise the LORD." So she named him Judah. Then Leah stopped having children. —Genesis 29:31–35

Leah just wanted one thing—her husband's love. With each child Leah bore, she hoped that this time, the child would draw her husband's heart toward her. But that one thing, no matter how deeply she longed for it, remained a solid "no" from the Lord. Are you in a similar situation? Have you prayed time and time again for God to fulfill a deep desire, only for it to go unfulfilled?

When we don't understand why God has said "no" to our requests, there are many ways we can respond. We can spiral into hopelessness, believing that God has forgotten us. We can put our hope in ourselves and try to manipulate outcomes. Or we can follow Leah's example. When her fourth child, Judah, was born, she shifted her eyes from her circumstances to the Lord and decided to hope in Him. You can almost see Leah opening her tightly grasped fist, breathing a sigh of surrender as she accepted what the Lord had given her.

Little did Leah know that it was through that fourth son Judah's line that Jesus would come. Forged in the fires of disappointment and grief was the beginning of the family line that led to our Savior. Like Leah, we may not understand the magnitude of God's work in and through our lives as we wrestle with unfulfilled desires. But when God says no, you can trust that His plan is good and He will redeem the painful parts of your story. Keep praying, keep hoping, but ultimately, put your hope not in your circumstances, but in the Lord of your circumstances.

Pray: *Lord, I don't understand why You've said no, but I choose to trust that Your plan for me is better than my plan for myself. Like the birth of Judah ultimately led to the birth of Jesus, bring purpose out of my pain that gives You glory.*

7: WHEN THERE'S NO END IN SIGHT

So Joseph's master took him and had him thrown into the prison where the king's prisoners were confined. While Joseph was there in the prison, the L*ORD* *was with him and extended kindness to him, granting him favor in the eyes of the prison warden.* —Genesis 39:20–21

In dark times, it can feel like someone has locked you in a jail cell and thrown away the key, condemning you to a prison sentence with no end date. The thought of another month or even another week in such circumstances is overwhelming, and the enemy tries to convince you that life will never be worth living again.

Joseph was also likely tempted to despair during his own time in prison. At the age of seventeen, this young man with a bright future was sold into Egyptian slavery by his brothers. There, he was wrongfully accused of rape and thrown into prison, where he would spend at least two years. With no end date to his prison sentence, Joseph may have wondered if he'd be there for the rest of his life. God showed him kindness and gave him favor with the warden, but in that dark place, he may still have felt like that God had forgotten him.

But God hadn't forgotten Joseph for a moment. In fact, while Joseph may have been wrestling with feelings of abandonment and hopelessness, God was working out a perfectly timed plan to raise him up for a great purpose. After some time in prison, Joseph was called before the pharaoh to interpret a dream. God enabled him to do so, and the pharaoh placed him as second in command shortly before famine ravaged the land. Joseph was then able to save God's people and his own family from starvation.

Are you losing hope because there is no end in sight? If you are only hanging on to hope by a thread, remember this: Just as God never left Joseph, He has never left you. Just as God was working out a beautiful purpose and future joy for Joseph, so He is working out your own beautiful testimony. Our Savior is *"the same yesterday and today and forever"* (Hebrews 13:8), and the God who worked in Joseph's life is the same God who is working in yours.

Pray: *Father, there is no end in sight to this struggle, and I want to give up. Help me to trust that just as You were working in Joseph's life during his imprisonment, You are working in mine. Holy Spirit, empower me to hope even when hope seems impossible and give me glimpses of the purposes You are preparing for me.*

8: WHEN IT'S RISKY TO DO WHAT IS RIGHT

Then the king of Egypt said to the Hebrew midwives, whose names were Shiphrah and Puah, "When you help the Hebrew women give birth, observe them on the birthstools. If the child is a son, kill him; but if it is a daughter, let her live." The midwives, however, feared God and did not do as the king of Egypt had instructed; they let the boys live. —Exodus 1:15–17

The book of Exodus opens with the account of two of the bravest women recorded in Scripture: Shiphrah and Puah. In defying the pharaoh's edict to kill the baby boys they delivered, they boldly risked their lives.

Your life may not be on the line, but you might be facing a situation where following God's commands is risky. Perhaps your supervisor is asking you to do something unethical, and if you refuse, she could make your life difficult. Maybe the Holy Spirit is prompting you to share about Jesus with someone who is hostile toward Christians. Perhaps you're tempted to tell a lie to save face. In each of these circumstances, you desire to do what is right but may feel you lack the courage to follow through. Shiphrah and Puah's courage may seem far beyond you, but the truth is *it's not.* They were ordinary women just like you, with fears, weakness, and anxieties. The source of their courage wasn't their own strength, but *fear of God.*

You can follow in Shiphrah and Puah's footsteps by fearing God rather than fearing the consequences of following Him. Fear of God is simply seeing and accepting reality for what it is: God is the only One worthy of honor and glory and praise. Human power—even that of a king—is no match for Him. Oswald Chambers put it well, saying, "The remarkable thing about fearing God is that when you fear God you fear nothing else, whereas if you do not fear God you fear everything else."[1] When you fear God, everything else comes into its proper perspective.

When you do the right thing despite the risks, you can't predict the outcome. You *can*, however, be confident that your faithfulness is precious to Him and that He will use it for His glory. Whatever you're facing, take courage as you reflect on Shiphrah and Puah's example, trusting that when you fear God, He will give you the courage to act according to His commands, whatever the outcome.

Pray: *Lord, I am facing a situation where it is risky to do what is right. Help me to see You as You are, that I may fear You and fear nothing else.*

9: WHEN YOU NEED TO TRUST GOD WITH YOUR FAMILY

Now a man of the house of Levi married a daughter of Levi, and she conceived and gave birth to a son. When she saw that he was a beautiful child, she hid him for three months. But when she could no longer hide him, she got him a papyrus basket and coated it with tar and pitch. Then she placed the child in the basket and set it among the reeds along the bank of the Nile. —Exodus 2:1–3

Jochebed did possibly the hardest thing for a mother to do; she let go of her precious baby, not knowing whether he would live or die. She did her best for him, but ultimately, she had to surrender him to God as she watched him slowly float away down the Nile. We know the outcome—Moses would survive and one day lead his people out of Egypt—but Jochebed didn't.

---

1. Oswald Chambers, *The Highest Good: The Shadow of an Agony* (Grand Rapids, MI: Discovery House, 1992), 148.

You may not have had to let go of your family as literally as Jochebed, but her faith can still encourage you to respond with trust when you are worried about them. Trusting God with your family is uniquely challenging. Whether you fear for a child's safety, are anxious about a sibling's mental health, or worry about your parents as they age, concern for your family can quickly spiral into full-blown fear because of your deep love and connection. Jochebed likely felt the same storm of emotions as she prepared the papyrus basket for Moses's escape, savoring those last moments with her son with a lump in her throat. Still, she let go of Moses in a courageous act of trust.

One of the hardest things we will do in this life is to unclench our fists and trust God with the family we hold so dear. The only way we can do this is by believing the truth that our family is safer in God's hands than in ours. He knows what they need, when they need it, and how to reach them. He knows the hairs on their heads, the numbers of their days, and the sorrows of their hearts. His love for them is immense, and you can trust that they are in good hands.

Pray: *Father, I am worried about my family, and I'm struggling to let go and believe that You will take care of them. May I follow Jochebed's example and entrust my family to You, confident that You will be with them whatever they face.*

10: WHEN YOU FEAR THE POWER OF THE ENEMY

And Balaam lifted up an oracle, saying: "Balak brought me from Aram, the king of Moab from the mountains of the east. 'Come,' he said, 'put a curse on Jacob for me; come and denounce Israel!' How can I curse what God has not cursed? How can I denounce what the LORD has not denounced?"
—Numbers 23:7–8

Many Christians fear the power of the enemy, constantly bracing themselves for demonic attacks and curses. As Christians, we do engage in spiritual battle, but God has equipped us with the armor we need (see Ephesians 6:10–17) and has promised to protect us from the evil one. (See 2 Thessalonians 3:3.) Although spiritual forces may *attack* us, they cannot *infiltrate* us, for we are filled with the Holy Spirit and sealed as His. We do not need to fear the power of the enemy because the all-powerful God is our Protector, Father, and King.

The account of Balaam in Numbers 22–23 shows that the forces of evil have no power over God's people. When the king of Moab commanded Balaam to prophesy a curse over Israel, the angel of the Lord stopped Balaam in his tracks, brandishing a sword and warning him to turn back from his evil journey. When Balaam admitted he had sinned, the angel allowed him to continue on the journey, but to say only what God told him. (See Numbers 22:35.) When the moment came to curse Israel, only words of blessing would come from Balaam's mouth! His best efforts were no match for God's fierce protection of His people. God controlled his very words.

You too, can be confident that the only true God, the resurrected One who has power over life and death, *also* has power over the enemy. Like Balaam learned, no one can curse what God has not cursed and no one can denounce what God has not denounced. As Jesus reassures His followers over one thousand years later, *"I give them eternal life, and they will never perish. No one can snatch them out of My hand"* (John 10:28). If you are His, you do not need to fear the enemy's power. God has equipped you, He is protecting you, and nothing can separate you from His love.

Pray: *Lord Jesus, I have feared the power of the enemy over my life, but because I am Yours, the enemy no longer has any power over me. In You, I am blessed, and in You, I am protected. Thank You that You have rescued me from darkness and that no one can snatch me out of Your hand!*

11: WHEN YOU WONDER IF FOLLOWING JESUS IS WORTH IT

But Ruth replied: "Do not urge me to leave you or to turn from following you. For wherever you go, I will go, and wherever you live, I will live; your people will be my people, and your God will be my God. Where you die, I will die, and there I will be buried. May the Lord *punish me, and ever so severely, if anything but death separates you and me."* —Ruth 1:16–17

Jesus tells us that our lives won't necessarily get any easier when we follow Him. He tells us that we must take up our cross and put Him above everything else. He tells us that if people hated Him, they will hate us too. When you consider the sacrifices you'll have to make, is following Jesus truly worth it?

The story of a young Moabite woman shows us that following Jesus is *more than worth it*. When Ruth's Jewish husband, brother-in-law, and father-in-law all passed away, her mother-in-law Naomi prepared to leave Moab and return to her people. Naomi urged Ruth to stay in Moab, find a new husband, and get a second chance at a happily ever after. Ruth's sister-in-law Orpah did just that, but Ruth stubbornly refused to leave Naomi.

What could have compelled Ruth to follow her mother-in-law into an unknown future? The answer is that she had tasted the goodness of the God of Abraham, Isaac, and Jacob. She saw that her people's gods were idols and that no earthly experience or hope could compare to following the Lord. Ruth counted the cost—she knew she might never marry, have a child, or be accepted by the people she was going live among. But when she counted the cost, she knew it was worth it.

Ruth didn't know that one day, she would bear a child who would be the grandfather of King David and the predecessor of the very Messiah she'd unknowingly set her hope on when she left her home behind. She had no way of knowing the joys to come, but she counted the joy of following the one true God the only thing she needed.

Ruth is proof that following Jesus is more than worth it. Any sacrifice you make because you are His follower pales in comparison to knowing Him, and any suffering you face for Him will be eclipsed by joy when you meet Him face to face.

Pray: *Jesus, following You is more than worth it. When I make sacrifices and suffer as Your follower, help me not to grow weary or cynical. May I experience the unshakable joy that comes from knowing You.*

12: WHEN YOU FEEL BITTER

Then the women said to Naomi, "Blessed be the LORD, who has not left you this day without a kinsman-redeemer. May his name become famous in Israel. He will renew your life and sustain you in your old age. For your daughter-in-law, who loves you and is better to you than seven sons, has given him birth." And Naomi took the child, placed him on her lap, and became a nurse to him. The neighbor women said, "A son has been born to Naomi," and they named him Obed. He became the father of Jesse, the father of David. —Ruth 4:14–17

Naomi had been dealt a tragic hand. Her husband and sons had died, and she was left with nothing. Many of us can empathize with her bitterness. She felt so bitter, in fact, that she took bitterness as a name. *"Do not call me Naomi,"* she said. *"Call me Mara, because the Almighty has dealt quite bitterly with me. I went away full, but the LORD has brought me back empty"* (Ruth 1:20–21). Whereas Naomi meant "pleasantness or sweetness," Mara meant "bitter." Bitterness was now central to her identity.

When Naomi called herself bitter, she couldn't imagine the sweetness God was going to bring into her life. She had no idea that her daughter-in-law would give birth to a baby who would not only bring joy to Naomi in her old age, but who would become King David's grandfather and be in the line of Christ!

Bitterness was never Naomi's true identity. Joy, not sorrow, would be her lasting legacy. The same is true for us. We will face sorrow in this life, but if we belong to Jesus, we know that sorrow doesn't have the last word.

Is there an area of your life where bitterness has become central to your identity? If so, reflect on how God replaced Naomi's bitterness with joy, and trust that God will redeem your suffering as well. Though your life may feel very bitter right now, God has *not* forgotten you, and He is working all things together for your good. (See Romans 8:28.)

Pray: *Lord, my life feels very bitter right now, and my bitterness has become a part of my identity. Give me Your perspective on this pain, that I may not find my identity in my bitterness, but in Your goodness and love.*

13: WHEN YOU'RE DISTRESSED

In her bitter distress, Hannah prayed to the LORD and wept with many tears. And she made a vow, pleading, "O LORD of Hosts, if only You will look upon the affliction of Your maidservant and remember me, not forgetting Your maidservant but giving her a son, then I will dedicate him to the LORD all the days of his life, and no razor shall ever come over his head."
—1 Samuel 1:10–11

Worn down by years of dashed hopes and constant taunting, Hannah was *bitterly distressed*. Like most Hebrew women, she'd likely dreamed of marital bliss and precious children filling her home. But year after year, her womb remained empty, and her husband's fertile second wife taunted her for her barrenness.

Can you see yourself in Hannah's story? Is there something you've been hoping for year after year, but your hands remain empty while others hold the blessings you've prayed for? If so, our sister Hannah offers a beautiful example of how we can run to the Lord in our bitter distress with both *boldness* and *humility*.

Hannah was *bold* as she poured her heart out to God. The Scripture doesn't paint a picture of a woman with a stiff upper lip who pretended she didn't care all that much. No, we see a woman who "*wept with many tears*" and pleaded with the Lord. Though she lived over one thousand years before the book of Hebrews was written, she gives an example of "*approach*[ing] *the throne of grace with confidence, so that we may receive mercy and find grace to help us in our time of need*" (Hebrews 4:16). You, too, can go to God with all your raw, unfiltered emotions. He is gracious, and He cares for you.

Hannah also approached the Lord with *humility*, twice calling herself the Lord's maidservant. Though she pled with the Lord, she did not demand anything from Him. By identifying as a maidservant, she reminded herself that God didn't owe her anything. He was not a servant to her will; she was a servant to His. When we plead with the Lord, may we also remember that we are the Lord's servant, and that His will is better than anything we could dream up.

When you are distressed, let Hannah's example remind you that God is gracious, kind, and trustworthy. Run to Him boldly and humbly, confident that He hears your prayers.

Pray: *Father, like Hannah, I am bitterly distressed. You know the longings of my heart and the pain I've lived through. You also know what is best for me. I surrender my longings to You, trusting that Your will for my life is good.*

14: WHEN YOU CULTIVATE DISCERNMENT

Then David said to Abigail, "Blessed be the Lord, the God of Israel, who sent you to meet me this day! Blessed is your discernment, and blessed are you, because today you kept me from bloodshed and from avenging myself by my own hand." —1 Samuel 25:32–33

Married to a man who was both foolish and evil, Abigail was living most women's nightmare. Despite her difficult circumstances, Abigail didn't allow Nabal's foolishness to rub off on her or his evil to intimidate her. In fact, she shows remarkable wisdom that saved the lives of many, leaving us an example of how God can use us when we cultivate discernment.

When David, the future king, requested refreshment from Nabal after he treated his men well, Nabal haughtily refused. Overcome by anger, David resolved to kill him and his men. Nabal's wife Abigail swooped in and saved the day. Hearing of David's plan, she acted fast, sending food ahead and running to meet him. Humbly bowing, she articulately advocated for her household's lives. Abigail's discerning words disarmed David and diffused his anger. Persuaded by Abigail's words, he saw that killing Nabal was not the answer and that God had kept him from shedding blood.

We don't know exactly how Abigail became so discerning, but it's fair to guess that living with a man like Nabal offered many opportunities to develop discernment. When David's anger flared, Abigail met that anger with coolheaded wisdom, and you can imagine she had already been through many similar scenarios with her husband. Although none of us would wish to be in Abigail's shoes, consider how growing in wisdom while she navigated difficult circumstances prepared her to act wisely in a life-or-death situation.

When we are faced with difficult circumstances and difficult people, we have the same choice as Abigail. Are we going to cultivate discernment, asking the Lord to teach and develop us through these situations? True wisdom comes from the Lord, and the more we seek Him, read His Word, and are faithful in the small things, the readier we will be for situations that require an extra dose of discernment. Let us pray that God develops us into women who, like Abigail, act with a cool head, godly wisdom, and a humble heart.

Pray: *Lord, may I not be discouraged by the foolishness and evil around me. Instead, help me to cultivate discernment in the trials I face that I may be ready when You call me to act.*

15: WHEN YOU'RE EXHAUSTED

Then [Elijah] *lay down under the broom tree and fell asleep. Suddenly an angel touched him and said, "Get up and eat." And he looked around, and there by his head was a cake of bread baked over hot coals, and a jar of water. So he ate and drank and lay down again. A second time the angel of the* Lord *returned and touched him, saying, "Get up and eat, or the journey will be too much for you." So he got up and ate and drank. And strengthened by that food, he walked forty days and forty nights until he reached Horeb, the mountain of* God. —1 Kings 19:5–8

Elijah wanted to die. Or so he thought. Although he had seen God's miraculous power firsthand, he was terrified of an uncertain future. The evil queen Jezebel had been murdering God's prophets left and right and was now determined to kill Elijah. God had used Elijah to humiliate the prophets of Baal and show Himself as the one true God (see 1 Kings 18), and Jezebel was furious. Fearing a violent death, Elijah pleaded with the Lord to take his life before the evil queen could find him. What was the point in living if only torment lay ahead? Overwhelmed with exhaustion from the constant battle, his weariness amplified a fear of the future and outshouted God's faithfulness in the past.

In his exhaustion, Elijah was just as vulnerable as we are to the dark thoughts that fight to kill the remembrance of God's faithfulness in our lives. But God did not condemn Elijah for giving into fear. Despite Elijah's unbelief, God showed him compassion, faithfulness, and love by giving him rest and nourishment to strengthen his mind and restore his hope. Instead of granting Elijah's plea for death, he sent an angel to give him food, water, and words of encouragement. (See 1 Kings 19.)

The Lord has compassion on your weakness and understands how exhaustion makes you especially vulnerable to hopelessness about your future. He is kind and gentle when you doubt that He will provide the rest you long for. Just as He did for Elijah, He will act on your behalf and give you just what you need to walk into the future. Your loving Father will meet you in your pain and lead you to a place of nourishment, rest, and hope.

Pray: *Lord, I am weary, and my mind is overwhelmed. I don't think I can take the next step, much less walk into the future. Please act on my behalf and give me the rest and nourishment my body and mind desperately need. Restore my mind and restore my hope.*

16: WHEN YOU FEEL ALONE IN YOUR FAITH

"I have been very zealous for the Lord, the God of Hosts," he replied, "but the Israelites have forsaken Your covenant, torn down Your altars, and killed Your prophets with the sword. I am the only one left, and they are seeking my life as well." —1 Kings 19:14

Does it ever seem like you're the only one following the Lord? Perhaps you're the only one in your family following Jesus, and you feel isolated, different, and misunderstood. Maybe you're in a workplace where coworkers routinely scoff at Christianity, and you're the butt of jokes. Or maybe you're struggling to find a church with sound teaching, and you long for fellowship with other believers.

Elijah was in a similar situation. He didn't doubt God's power—He had just seen Him rain down fire on a soaking-wet altar to show up the prophets of Baal. He had experienced God's care—the Lord had revived him when he despaired of life. Still, his fear remained, as he was convinced that all other followers of the Lord had been killed, and he was next.

The Lord surprises Elijah by telling him that he was wrong—he was *not* the only one left. In fact, there were many still committed to the Lord. He told Elijah, *"I have reserved seven thousand in Israel—all whose knees have not bowed to Baal and whose mouths have not kissed him"* (1 Kings 19:18).

Elijah's belief that he was alone was based on his limited perspective—he could not currently see the thousands of other believers separating themselves from Baal worship. In God's kindness, he broke through Elijah's human understanding with the truth that he was not alone!

This is true for you as well. Although you may be in a season where you feel alone in your faith, there are still many who follow the Lord. Pray for the Lord to bring other believers into your life, but in the meantime, know that there are others just like you. As you walk through this season of solitary faith, pray for your brothers and sisters around the world who feel alone, trusting that God will make your paths cross when the time is right.

Pray: *Lord, I feel alone in my faith. I have seen Your goodness and am committed to following You, but sometimes this journey feels so lonely. Please bring other believers into my life in Your timing and strengthen believers around the world who are also feeling alone in their faith.*

17: WHEN YOU'RE AFRAID

Truly, O Lord, the kings of Assyria have laid waste these nations and their lands. They have cast their gods into the fire and destroyed them, for they were not gods, but only wood and stone—the work of human hands. And now, O Lord our God, please save us from his hand, so that all the kingdoms of the earth may know that You alone, O Lord, are God.
—2 Kings 19:17–19

When you're afraid, the solution isn't to minimize your problems or pretend they don't exist, but to set your eyes on the One who is far greater than the object of your fear.

King Hezekiah had reason to fear the king of Assyria's threats. Not only had he seen what Assyria had done to other peoples, but the king sent emissaries to tell Hezekiah's people not to listen when he told them to trust in the Lord. (See verses 9–13.) They had the receipts for why they shouldn't trust in the Lord—after all, Assyria had crushed the surrounding nations. Trusting in the Lord would be foolish.

Hezekiah never denied that he had a reason to be afraid. In fact, he acknowledged that Assyria *was* powerful and *had* crushed other nations. He even went so far as to tear his clothes! (See verse 1.) However, he then looked to God's power, refusing to entertain the lies of the king's emissaries. The other nations had been crushed, but it was because their gods were only idols who had no power to protect. They had nothing on the one true God. Seeing through the lens of truth, Hezekiah humbly appealed to the Lord. We can and should do the same.

Like Hezekiah, you may face very real threats, and you don't need to deny their reality. Instead, choose to tune out the lies of the enemy and pray to the Lord in full confidence. He is not like the gods of other nations or the idols of our own culture, which have no power to save. He is more powerful than the most powerful threat on earth, and you don't need to be afraid.

Pray: *Lord, I am facing real threats, and I am afraid. Everything and everyone around me tells me not to trust You, but I know that You are trustworthy, good, and far more powerful than any evil that comes against me. Fill me with courage and trust as I wait on You.*

18: WHEN YOU'RE IN AN IMPOSSIBLE SITUATION

We are powerless before this vast army that comes against us. We do not know what to do, but ***our eyes are upon You.*** —2 Chronicles 20:12

Are you facing a situation that seems impossible? Whether your impossible battle involves relationships, mental health, finances, or something else, we have all faced things we can't overcome on our own. For many of us, our first response is fear that unless we put in maximum effort, God will not act on our behalf. Our culture has fed us the lie that "God helps those who help themselves," and we treat that trite aphorism like gospel truth, traveling our minds in desperation, feet pounding the well-worn pathways of anxiety, eyes scanning the horizon for an answer. But our travels only yield sore feet and the bleeding of hope from long-open wounds. We are running in circles, and we need to stop.

When you find yourself in a frenzy, trying to figure things out, remember how God delivered His people from an enemy far stronger than them. When faced with almost certain defeat, King Jehoshaphat spoke a simple yet profound declaration of trust in the Lord: "*We do not know what to do, but our eyes are upon You*" (2 Chronicles 20:12).

King Jehoshaphat didn't frantically rally his army, believing that God would only help him if he helped himself. Instead, he humbly acknowledged that he had no idea what to do, and that the only thing that would save him was God's wisdom. The Lord responded, saying, "*The battle does not belong to you, but to God*" (2 Chronicles 20:15). God then miraculously fought the battle for His people, causing their enemies to be ambushed and then to destroy each other.

In the same way, when you are facing an impossible situation, the battle is not yours to fight. You do not have to convince God that you are trying hard enough in order to receive His help. It may not seem like it right now, but you are blessed when your strength is small, your vision is poor, and your ability is meager. For when the path clears before you, you'll know it was God's wisdom and not your conspiring, God's strength and not your striving.

Whatever impossible situation you are facing, shift your eyes from your circumstances on to the Lord and marvel as He takes your hand and leads you to freedom in His way and in His timing.

Pray: *Lord, I don't know what to do in this situation, but my eyes are on You. You are the source of wisdom and strength, and I trust You to guide my steps and act on my behalf.*

19: WHEN YOUR LIFE TAKES AN UNEXPECTED TURN

For if you remain silent at this time, relief and deliverance for the Jews will arise from another place, but you and your father's house will perish. And who knows if perhaps you have come to the kingdom for such a time as this?
—Esther 4:14

In improvisational comedy, there's a principle called "yes, and." In the middle of a skit, you never question what your co-actor does; you say *yes* to the new reality, *and* you build off of it. If he says, "I hate this Georgia heat," you don't say, "You're crazy! It's winter, and we're in Maine." No, you tell him it sounds like it's time for some sweet tea. To refuse to say "yes, and" breaks the flow of the story and puts the focus on you, the actor, rather than on your character.

Saying *yes, and* when things don't go as planned doesn't come naturally. We each have a *perfect plan* for our lives, and when things don't go our way, we often sulk and get angry at God rather than saying yes to what He's calling us to. But ... when we dare to say *yes, and*, we say yes to the best opportunity possible—joining God in the adventure of advancing His kingdom.

Queen Esther gave one of the most powerful *yes, ands* in history. She likely expected to marry a Jewish man and live in relative simplicity, but God had other plans and made her queen of Persia. This wasn't an easy road—taken from her home by the king's edict, she had no choice in the matter. She could, however, choose how to respond. Her uncle Mordecai challenged her to say *yes, and* to her God-given situation when he said,

"Perhaps you have come to the kingdom for such a time as this." Esther took Mordecai's words to heart, and God used Esther mightily to save many of her people from death.

You probably haven't been ripped from your home to become queen, but your life may not be what you expected either. In the unexpected, have the courage to be like Esther and say, "Yes, and." Look to the Lord, ask Him what's next, and embrace your new reality. You can trust that just as He called Esther to the throne for a reason, He has called you to this season for a good and holy purpose.

Pray: *Father, I'm struggling to accept that life hasn't gone as I'd planned, but in this moment, I say "yes, and" to the life You've called me to. Open my eyes to Your goodness in this unexpected season and help me to act wisely, trusting that I have been called to this place for a purpose.*

20: WHEN YOU FEEL FAR FROM GOD

If I go east, He is not there, and if I go west, I cannot find Him. When He is at work in the north, I cannot behold Him; when He turns to the south, I cannot see Him. Yet He knows the way I have taken; when He has tested me, ***I will come forth as gold.*** —Job 23:8–10

If you've ever felt far from God, the enemy can tempt you to self-condemn. One of his most insidious points of entry is through well-intentioned words that twist Scripture. The popular saying, "If you feel far from God, guess who moved?" can be especially discouraging.

If you've heard this from a friend, mentor, or pastor, you may have been disturbed by the implication that feeling distant from God means you have rebelled and run from Him. By this definition, your feelings are your reality; if you feel far from God, you must be far from Him. Yet Scripture tells us the opposite about the connection between our feelings and God's closeness. God doesn't tell us that our feelings create our reality; instead He says we need to trust Him because our understanding is limited and flawed. (See Proverbs 3:5–6.)

Your feelings are not a measure of your devotion to Jesus nor are they a barometer of God's closeness. If you have trusted in Jesus as your Savior, nothing can separate you from His love—even the darkest of feelings. (See Romans 8:38–39.) When you feel far from God, do not condemn yourself. Instead, stubbornly cling to His promises.

Job's poetic words show a tenacious faith not swayed by feelings. Job lamented how he sought God in every direction yet still couldn't feel His love or discern what He was doing. He follows his lament with a truth that defied his feelings—that God knew his path and would use his trials to refine and beautify him.

You can be confident that God will do the same for you, acting on your behalf even when you can't see it and holding you close even when you don't feel it. Nothing can separate you from His love, not even your feelings.

Pray: *Lord, I feel far from You. You say You will never leave me or forsake me, and You always keep Your promises. Like Job, I declare in faith that You know my way and will refine me through this season, bringing me forth as gold, a shining beacon of Your glory and grace. May I trust in You and not in my feelings.*

21: WHEN YOU CONSIDER YOUR INMOST THOUGHTS

May the words of my mouth and the meditation of my heart be pleasing in Your sight, O LORD, my Rock and my Redeemer. —Psalm 19:14

What is your inner monologue like? Although most of your thoughts will never be spoken aloud, they make up the majority of your inner life. Others may not hear your thoughts, but your thoughts still matter greatly.

The Lord calls us to live with integrity, for our inner and outer selves to match. Many of us, though, struggle to align our inner thoughts and outward actions. Those around you may think you are the kindest, most patient woman in the world, but your inner monologue may be impatient and critical. Others may compliment you for your servant's heart, but you know, deep down, that you grumble each time you have to pick up someone else's slack. We all struggle with negative thoughts, but there is hope. If you notice themes of complaining, envy, lust, or anything sinful in your inner monologue, the Lord wants to renew your mind and increase your integrity.

Our minds are a battlefield, but the Lord has given us a powerful weapon—*"the sword of the Spirit, which is the word of God"* (Ephesians 6:17). If you are a follower of Jesus, the Holy Spirit lives in you and will transform your inner monologue as you bathe your mind in Scripture. David's prayer in Psalm 19 is a powerful passage to wield against the enemy and the flesh's desire to control your mind; it both orients your mind to pleasing the Lord in your thoughts and calls on His power for help.

As you consider your inner monologue over the next several days, take heart if the Holy Spirit convicts you that it needs to change. Do not be alarmed at the patterns that have taken root. Simply come to the Lord, confident of His grace, and ask Him to transform your mind as you think about His Word. He will finish the work He has started in you. (See Philippians 1:6.)

Pray: *Lord, I want to grow in integrity and Christlikeness of thought. Holy Spirit, bring the Word of God to my mind as I go throughout my day. May the words of my mouth and the meditation of my heart be pleasing in Your sight, O Lord, my Rock and my Redeemer.*

22: WHEN YOU'RE TRUSTING IN YOUR RESOURCES

A horse is a vain hope for salvation; even its great strength cannot save. Surely the eyes of the Lord are on those who fear Him, on those whose hope is in His loving devotion to deliver them from death and keep them alive in famine. —Psalm 33:17–19

Hoping in a horse sounds odd to modern ears, but David Guzik explains, "Horses were some of the most advanced military tools in that day."[2] It was essential to be outfitted with strong, fit horses to win a war. Without horses, an army would be rendered powerless.

Horses themselves may not be culturally relevant, but they represent our tendency to trust in human resources to meet our needs and solve our problems. Cutting-edge technologies promise to make our lives easier and even fulfill the desires of our hearts. Want to make money? There's an investment app for that. Longing to meet the love of your life? They might just be a few swipes away. The problem lies not in investing or online dating, but in putting our *trust* in those things. If you find yourself saying, "If I don't use this app, there's no chance I'll meet someone," you're hoping in a horse. When you think, "I have to devise the perfect retirement strategy, or I'll be destitute when I'm older," you're hoping in a horse.

When we hope in a horse, we forget God's sovereignty in the equation of our lives. When we hope in a horse, we say that we have to control things because we don't believe God will. This passage puts things in the right perspective. Hoping in a horse is vain, but hoping in the Lord is powerful. In many Old Testament accounts, God saved His people from their enemies when they were unequipped and outnumbered. There were also many times that Israel was well equipped, but because their hearts weren't right with God, they were defeated.

Whether we have an abundance of *horses* or none, it doesn't matter. What matters is that whether we have much or little, we put our hope in the Lord. Our resources are finite and may fail, but our God loves us deeply and has never failed.

Pray: *Lord, I confess that I have trusted in many horses. I have put my hope in my resources rather than Your sovereignty. I put my hope in Your great love for me, and I trust You to guide and sustain me.*

---

2. David Guzik, "Psalm 33: The Great and Awesome God," Enduring Word Bible Commentary, enduringword.com/bible-commentary/psalm-33.

23: WHEN YOUR DESIRES GO UNFULFILLED

Delight yourself in the LORD, and He will give you the desires of your heart.
—Psalm 37:4

This is one of the most misused verses in the church today. It is often used to claim a blank check from God for our earthly desires. Follow Jesus, and He'll give you a perfect marriage, healthy children, financial prosperity, and the fulfillment of your dreams. But when we put this verse in the context of the whole biblical narrative, we see something different play out in the lives of many who delighted themselves in the Lord.

Job delighted himself in the Lord, but he lost his children and his health.

The apostle Paul delighted himself in the Lord, yet he was plagued by *"a thorn in my flesh"* that wasn't removed even after he pleaded three times for its removal. (See 2 Corinthians 12:7–9.)

Jesus, God incarnate, delighted Himself in the Lord, yet He dreaded the cross and asked the Father if there was another way.

When we look at Job, Paul, and our risen Lord, it's clear that the American interpretation of Psalm 37:4 contradicts the lives of many who had a close relationship with God.

So what does it mean that God will fulfill out heart's desires when we delight ourselves in Him? Alexander Maclaren cautions us, "Do not vulgarise that great promise by making it out to mean that, if we will be good, He will give us the earthly blessings which we wish. Sometimes we shall get them, and sometimes not; but our text goes far deeper than that. God Himself is the heart's desire of those who delight in Him; and the blessedness of longing fixed on Him is that it ever fulfils itself."[3]

Vulgarize is a strong word, but it's an apt description of what we do when we view satisfaction in Christ as a means to an end. God offers us

---

3. Alexander Maclaren, *Expositions of Holy Scripture, Vol. 3, The Psalms, Isaiah 1-48* (Grand Rapids, MI: W. B. Eerdmans Publishing Co., 1959), 256.

Himself, but we often run past His open arms as we greedily search for His gifts. Following Christ should never be a means to an end; following Christ should be our chief end. The next time you hear Psalm 37:4, instead of fixating on an earthly desire, take a moment to delight in the Lord who loves you, redeemed you, and is preparing an eternal place for you. He is worth immeasurably more than all your earthly desires, and He wants to become the desire of your heart.

Pray: *Father, make knowing You the chief desire of my heart! May I never make following You a means to an end but may it become my delight.*

24: WHEN YOU'RE AFRAID OF MAKING THE WRONG DECISION

The steps of a man are ordered by the LORD who takes delight in his journey. Though he falls, he will not be overwhelmed, for the LORD is holding his hand. —Psalm 37:23–24

When you're making a big decision, have you ever felt like God was hiding the right answer from you? For many Christians, seeking God's will is a fear-ridden game of trivia, where there is one *right* answer and one *wrong* answer. If you happen to make the wrong choice, you fear your life will be ruined, and God will look on in indifference, saying, "You made your bed; now lie in it." Seeking God's will in this way may be common, but it's not biblical. Scripture doesn't say that He delights in seeing us strive and fail, but that He delights in each step of our journey.

We should seek God and get godly counsel when making decisions, but we don't need to fear making the *wrong* decision. We please God not by agonizing over the *right* decision, but by using the wisdom He gives to make a *godly* decision. Every decision comes with risk, and when difficulties follow our decision, we may question whether we acted in line with God's will. But if you make a decision with an open heart toward God and surrender to His lordship, you do not need to fear that your difficulties are punishment for your choice. Many difficulties are simply the result of living in a fallen world. In John 16:33, Jesus tells His disciples that they will have trouble in this world, but that He has overcome it. The same is true for us. Making decisions within God's will isn't about avoiding pain but about honoring Him. When you do face difficulties, the Lord is not far off. As Psalm 37:24 says, "*Though he falls, he will not be overwhelmed, for the* L*ORD is holding his hand.*"

The next time you have to make a big decision, focus on God's delight in your journey and His unchanging presence in your life. If you are seeking God in your decision-making, you do not need to fear making the wrong decision. Whatever path you take, He is already there, ordering your steps, lighting your path, your steady constant in an ever-changing life.

Pray: *Father, I am afraid of making the wrong decision, but I know that You are for me, not against me. I ask for wisdom in this situation and courage to move forward. I know You will be with me, holding my hand, whatever comes.*

25: WHEN YOUR HEART FAILS

My flesh and my heart may fail, but ***God is the strength of my heart*** *and my portion forever.* —Psalm 73:26

How comforting that our faith is not dependent on our feelings! Our hearts fail, and they fail *often*. Our hearts fail to see things clearly; they doubt God's goodness although we know He's good. Our hearts fail to find joy in the Lord because the surrounding circumstances outshout what we know to be true. Our hearts fail to set their hope on knowing Christ and eternity with Him when the present trials and responsibilities seem much more pressing. Our hearts fail to believe that we are forgiven from our sins, and we spend our days in needless guilt and shame. Our hearts fail … but praise God that His commitment to us doesn't.

When we are weak and especially aware of our sinfulness, our hearts may fail, even fearing for our salvation. First John 3:20 comforts us in such moments with these words: "*Even if our hearts condemn us, God is greater than our hearts, and He knows all things.*" He knows our frailties. He knows the fluctuations of our hormones. He knows the traumas we've undergone and the struggles we face every day. He has saved us by His grace, not because of how we feel or what we can do. If we have trusted in Jesus as our Lord and Savior, our salvation is sure, and we can rest in Him.

Psalm 73:26 tells us that when our flesh and heart fail, God is the strength of our heart. He is the one who keeps us going, keeps us walking heavenward, keeps producing fruit in our lives, keeps encouraging and empowering us. When your heart fails you, may you remember that the Christian faith is not one of works but of trust and grace. Whether you're in a season of doubt, depression, anxiety, or recovery from trauma, He is your strength. He is for you, not against you, the sustainer of your life and perfecter of your faith.

Pray: *Lord, my heart is failing me. I don't feel my faith, and I need Your strength. Replace the lies that are attacking my heart with Your truth. When I feel You are far, remind me that You're with me. When I fear for my salvation, remind me that I've been saved by Your grace. My heart fails, but You never do.*

26: WHEN YOU ARE DISTRESSED

When I remember You on my bed, I think of You through the watches of the night. For You are my help; I will sing for joy in the shadow of Your wings. My soul clings to You; Your right hand upholds me. —Psalm 63:6–8

David wrote Psalm 63 in the direst of straits—while in the wilderness fleeing from King Saul or from David's own son Absalom, both of whom were plotting to kill him. Not only was David's life in danger, but he felt the emotional turmoil of being betrayed. Still, David didn't despair but penned a psalm of praise and trust in the Lord. His psalm provides a beautiful pattern for us to follow in similar times of turmoil: remember, sing, and cling.

In David's distress, he *remembers* God on sleepless nights, recounting how the Lord has helped him in the past. When the fear rose up,

David remembered how God had protected him in similar situations. In your current trial, can you remember a specific time God helped you in your troubles? Let that memory of God's faithfulness in the past bolster your faith in Him in the present.

David also *sings* to the Lord for joy. Joy may seem out of place in such a difficult situation, but David knew that he had a reason for joy because of the Lord's great love. Defiant against the powers of darkness, David penned the very psalm you are reading. You too can follow in David's footsteps by singing a song that praises the Lord. This act of defiance against the darkness is a beautiful act of faith.

Finally, David *clings* to the Lord. He knows that the Lord is his only hope for salvation. He cannot outrun or outsmart Saul or Absalom in his own strength. In the same way, do not try to rescue yourself. Do not try to do things on your own. God is the same God today as He was when He comforted and helped King David. In the words of Hebrews 13:8, *"Jesus Christ is the same yesterday and today and forever."* As you remember His faithfulness, sing to Him in your distress and cling to Him for dear life. You will see His goodness and love, whatever comes.

Pray: *Father, I feel like King David, distressed by attack and betrayal. Bring to mind memories of Your faithfulness, give me a new song, and help me to cling to You.*

27: WHEN YOU NEED REST

Unless the LORD builds the house, its builders labor in vain; unless the LORD protects the city, its watchmen stand guard in vain. In vain you rise early and stay up late, toiling for bread to eat—for He gives sleep to His beloved.
—Psalm 127:1–2

Do you believe the Lord wants to give you rest?

For many of us, our lips say *yes* to this question, but our lives say *no.* Faced with a mountain of tasks and responsibilities, there simply aren't enough hours in the day. If you need to cut something out of your schedule, it will be sleep. Your family is depending on you. You need this job. You'll disappoint many if you don't follow through. In short, your heart believes that if you rest, then your life and the lives of those around you will unravel.

May this psalm remind you that you do not hold your life or the lives of your loved ones together. God is your sustainer. He is the one who provides for you and your family. He has everything in His hands. And He has designed you to need rest.

Sometimes going to sleep is one of the greatest acts of trust in God. During those moments of unconsciousness while your mind is refreshed and your body restored, you have no illusion of control. When you wake up, you can worship the God who held everything together without you. Your very design speaks to the fact that you are dependent on God for your every breath. In order to live, you need sleep. Sleep is not a luxury, but a necessity.

Yet God is always awake, always watching over you. Psalm 121:4 says, *"Behold, the Protector of Israel will neither slumber nor sleep."* What a contrast between God and His people! You, who must sleep, can trust in Him, while He, who never sleeps, watches over you.

No matter how big your responsibilities are or how long your to-do list, remember that you are not your own sustainer. God is. He invites you to lie down and sleep while He watches over you.

Pray: *Lord, there doesn't seem to be enough time for sleep, but I am so weary. You invite me to rest, and You tell me that You are the only one who doesn't slumber or sleep. You give sleep to those You love; thank You for loving me and giving me the freedom to rest.*

28: WHEN YOU'RE LOOKING FOR A SIGN

For the Lord gives wisdom; from His mouth come knowledge and understanding. He stores up sound wisdom for the upright; He is a shield to those who walk with integrity, to guard the paths of justice and protect the way of His saints. —Proverbs 2:6–8

When faced with a big decision, have you ever asked God for a sign to confirm you're making the right choice? The desire for a sign is natural because as humans, we crave certainty. We also want to avoid pain. In seeking a sign, we may assume that God's stamp of approval on our choice will guarantee a painless road ahead. There are biblical examples of God giving His people signs, but these are the exception, not the rule. But the rule is even better! Though God doesn't promise to give us a sign, He *does* promise to give us wisdom.

What is the difference between a sign and wisdom? A sign is a *yes* or *no* that doesn't account for the situational data. Wisdom enables you to see a situation accurately, rightly discerning the data through the lens of God's Word. If you're asking for a sign about whether to marry your boyfriend yet he is consistently unkind to you and cold toward the Lord, you don't need a sign. God's wisdom is already beckoning you from the pages of His Word, asking you to consider whether this man lives up to God's definition of love (see 1 Corinthians 13) or exhibits the fruit of the Holy Spirit. (See Galatians 5:22–23.) The wisdom from God's Word warns you that this man will not be a godly husband. No sign is necessary.

The next time you have to make a big decision, instead of asking for a sign, ask for wisdom.

God loves giving wisdom and He does so generously. He doesn't hide it from you but *stores it up* for you. His Word is the very definition of wisdom, a storehouse of counsel and insight in your time of need. When you are a follower of Christ, the Holy Spirit indwells you and convicts, leads, and protects you with godly discernment. God has lavishly equipped you to make wise decisions that produce good fruit.

Pray: *Father, thank You for the wisdom You have stored up for me in Your Word. As I make difficult decisions, illuminate Your Word and enable me to see my situation through Your eyes, that I may honor You in all I do.*

29: WHEN YOU'RE LEANING ON YOUR OWN UNDERSTANDING

Trust in the Lord *with all your heart, and lean not on your own understanding; in all your ways acknowledge Him, and He will make your paths straight.* —Proverbs 3:5–6

Leaning is a great metaphor for trust. We only lean on what we believe can hold us up. We wouldn't lean against a fence that looked unstable, nor would we sit in a chair that was missing a leg.

When we struggle to trust God, we are often leaning on our own understanding. We view our perception as the sturdiest of fences while denouncing God's as a creaky fence about to collapse. Our view of how things should play out seems ironclad, and we place our full weight on our limited knowledge, creating a strategy for action based on what we see.

Our understanding, however, is the true tottering fence. As soon as we put our full weight on it, it falls, and we fall along with it. We might fall into despair when a child walks away from the Lord and we don't know what to do. We might fall into bitterness when the chronic health struggle gets worse and we don't understand why God hasn't healed us. We might fall into doubt that God loves us when years go by without an answer to our prayer that God would provide a spouse.

When we lean on our own understanding, we inevitably fall. God has given us wonderfully intricate minds, but there are gaps to our understanding, and those gaps are often biggest in matters of the heart. God is the only one with the understanding that can bear the weight of our stories. He knows everything about our situation while we only have a sliver of knowledge. He knows the beginning from the end and is actively involved in bringing good out of even the most painful situations.

The next time you catch yourself leaning on your own understanding, dare to trust in the Lord. When you lean on Him, you lean on something with the structural integrity to bear the heaviest of cares. He will guide you, making clear what was blurry and making your winding paths straight.

Pray: *Lord, Your knowledge is beyond human comprehension, and You understand my life so much better than I do. When I lean on my own understanding, I fall, but when I lean on You, I don't need to fear falling. As I trust in You, calm my mind, encourage my heart, and guide my steps.*

30: WHEN YOU'RE AFRAID OF THE FUTURE

Strength and honor are her clothing, and she can laugh at the days to come.
—Proverbs 31:25

When we consider the future, laughing is the last thing most of us do. Our knee-jerk reaction to the unknown is often worry and fear. If things are difficult, we may fear they'll never get better. If things are going well, we may brace ourselves for the other shoe to drop. As humans with the instinct for self-preservation, it's anything but natural to look toward the future without fear.

How does the woman of noble character laugh without fear of the future? The answer isn't that she has no fear at all, but that she fears *God*. A few verses later, we read of her, *"Charm is deceptive and beauty is fleeting, but a woman who fears the* Lord *is to be praised"* (verse 30). The future may objectively be frightening, but the Proverbs 31 woman knows that with the all-powerful Creator by her side, she doesn't need to fear anything.

Fear of the future can be a kind of counterfeit worship. We are wired to fear and worship God, and when our hearts are set on His power, love, and goodness, fear of the future loses its hold on us. When we don't fear God—whether we deliberately rebel or simply live in indifference toward Him—our wiring for fear has to manifest somewhere. This is often where fear of the future becomes its own type of worship, where we believe the future holds supreme control over us. In the future we imagine, we are almost always alone, and we frantically plan and strategize to make sure we are provided for. That's nothing to laugh at.

When we choose to fear the Lord, though, we can be confident we will never be alone. He has promised to be with us, and He has promised to provide. If you're struggling with fear when you consider the future, look back and remember how God has been faithful in the past. He is the same God yesterday as He is today, and you can approach an unknown future with laughter because of who is holding your hand. To paraphrase the apostle Paul in Romans 8:38–39, nothing, not even the future, can separate you from the love of God!

Pray: *Father, I am fearful as I look toward the future. Teach me to fear You, not the future, that I may laugh at the days to come.*

31: WHEN YOU DON'T FEEL BEAUTIFUL

Charm is deceptive and beauty is fleeting, but a woman who fears the LORD *is to be praised.* —Proverbs 31:30

Americans spend billions of dollars on beauty products every year. Why on earth would we spend this kind of money on lipstick, mascara, and moisturizer? One of the reasons beneath this shocking number is *fear.* Throughout the millennia, a woman's beauty has been seen a barometer for her worth and desirability. If we could be more beautiful, we think, we would be more loved, more cherished, more worthy. Our pursuit of beauty is often punctuated by fear because we know we're ultimately fighting a losing battle. The promise of earthly beauty has failed for every single woman throughout history.

Proverbs 31:30 gives us a powerful counterpoint to the fear inherent in the pursuit of physical beauty. We are not meant to frantically strive for physical attractiveness, which ultimately fades, but to fear the Lord—to shift our gaze from the mirror to His beauty, which never fades.

Robert Murray M'Cheyne said, "For every look at yourself, take ten looks at Christ." In our selfie-obsessed, mirror-saturated culture, this is a formula for freedom from fear. When we look at Jesus more than at ourselves, our perspective widens and our spiritual senses sharpen. When we look at Jesus more than at ourselves, beauty will take its rightful place in our lives. We will be more concerned with God's definition of beauty. Whereas worldly beauty fades, godly beauty grows with age. Godly beauty lies not in how you look, but simply in that you look to Him. True beauty is not flawless skin or a symmetrical face or hourglass figure. True beauty is in gazing upon our beautiful Lord. With our eyes fixed on the Lord rather than on our mirrors, we will experience a freedom that few women know.

With each year that our youthful beauty unravels, we don't need to fear, because those years bring us closer to the One we love and live for. The more we look at Him, the broader our vision will become, and we will no longer be deceived by our culture's fearful worship of appearance.

Pray: *Father, the world's definition of beauty fills me with anxiety and fear. The world tells me that physical beauty will be my savior, but this is a lie. Renew my mind as I gaze on Your beauty.*

32: WHEN YOU WONDER IF GOD CARES

Lift up your eyes on high: who created all these? He leads forth the starry host by number; He calls each one by name. Because of His great power and mighty strength, not one of them is missing. Why do you say, O Jacob, and why do you assert, O Israel, "My way is hidden from the Lord, and my claim is ignored by my God"? Do you not know? Have you not heard? The Lord is the everlasting God, the Creator of the ends of the earth. He will not grow tired or weary; His understanding is beyond searching out.

—Isaiah 40:26–28

Does the thought that God cares for you seem too good to be true? The Scriptures tell us again and again that God knows each of us personally, but with our limited human minds, this can be hard to believe. The idea that God knows each person defies human understanding, so in the midst of long trials or seemingly unanswered prayers, many of us have wondered if He truly cares. But what God spoke to His people through the prophet

Isaiah millennia ago is just as true for you today! God's understanding is so far beyond ours that He truly *can* and *does* care for each person.

Isaiah tells us what to do when we doubt that God cares—*look up.* Don't look at your troubles. Don't look at the circumstances that are insurmountable in human strength. Look up at the stars He created and be amazed. Since creation, the stars have pointed people to God's glory, awed them beyond their understanding, and put life in perspective, all because they are concrete evidence of a Creator whose ways are so vast and mighty that all the troubles and trappings of Earth pale in comparison. Look up and consider that just as He calls out each magnificent star by name, He knows your name and hears your cries.

He doesn't disregard your struggles—He is working all things for your good. (See Romans 8:28.) And one day, you will look back with clarity and awe at the constellation of His work in your life, as brilliant as His stars against the dark night sky.

Pray: *Lord, I stand in awe of how You care for me personally. Just as You created and know each star by name, You created me and know my name. I put my faith in Your love, and I trust that You are working in my life.*

33: WHEN SIN SEEMS BEAUTIFUL

To whom will you liken God? To what image will you compare Him? To an idol that a craftsman casts and a metalworker overlays with gold and fits with silver chains? —Isaiah 40:18–19

It's striking how intentionally the Israelites beautified their idols, idols that were ugly, inanimate, and powerless. Although we may not fashion and beautify physical idols today, we can do the same thing with sin, romanticizing it and convincing ourselves that it's beautiful. We are good at deceiving ourselves that our sin is not sin, casting thoughts and actions for our own glory in a noble light. It could be perfectionism, saying you are working your tail off for the Lord, but really doing it to prove your own worth. It could be playing the martyr, giving and serving to the point of exhaustion, secretly resenting how much people take you for granted. It could be building a social media platform, convincing yourself it's to advance the gospel when it's really motivated by a desire for affirmation. The common denominator in these examples is a focus on self. In these sins, we are the stars of our own movies.

We think being the leading lady would give us a life of beauty, adventure, and meaning. Instead, we are left feeling sad, defeated, and empty when we put ourselves in God's rightful place. It is when we take ourselves off the throne and stop trying to take God's place that our lives become full of the beauty, adventure, and meaning we long for. This is not easy. In fact, it's impossible on our own! But as followers of Christ, we don't have to do it in our own strength. Romans 8:9 tells us, *"You, however, are controlled not by the flesh, but by the Spirit, if the Spirit of God lives in you."*

When you find yourself beautifying your sin, putting yourself on the throne of your life, call on the Holy Spirit to help you in your weakness. The Holy Spirit will put your sin in its place and enable you to stand in awe of your Creator. He will open your eyes to the truth: nothing and no one can compare to Him.

Pray: *Father, I confess that I have beautified my sin, deceiving myself that I was acting nobly, when I've really just been putting myself in Your place. Holy Spirit, help me to see Your beauty. Strike me with the truth that nothing and no one compares to the Lord.*

34: WHEN YOU FEEL SHATTERED

O afflicted city, lashed by storms, without solace, surely I will set your stones in antimony and lay your foundations with sapphires. I will make your pinnacles of rubies, your gates of sparkling jewels, and all your walls of precious stones. —Isaiah 54:11–12

In the Japanese art of *kintsugi*, broken pottery is fused together with lacquer dusted with gold, creating a unique piece even more beautiful than the original. This metaphor is often used to describe how God redeems and repairs the broken pieces of our lives, beautifying them with His strength and healing. *But what if your life has been shattered?* What if the broken pieces are too small to glue together, some even pulverized into fine dust? What if the brokenness of your life is beyond restoration in its current form—a marriage ended, a trauma you can't unlive, horrific abuse, a loved one lost? As you look at the remnants of your former life, there is nothing to rebuild with.

Praise God that His work goes far beyond *kintsugi*. He doesn't need neatly broken pieces to do His work. He is a master craftsman with the richest of materials, and He has the means to rebuild your life as something completely new with the costliest of stones. In Isaiah 54:11–12, God describes His people as beyond comfort, beaten down by storms. No human intervention could restore them to their former wholeness. God declares He will go beyond restoring them to their former state—He will rebuild them with new and costly jewels. The cost of all the rubies and sapphires needed to rebuild a city were beyond human means, and the quantity was arguably more than even existed, but the Lord is never in short supply of the materials He uses to rebuild us.

Will you dare to believe that God wants to rebuild your life with new walls, new rooms, new windows created from precious stones? Notice that He says *"surely,"* He *will* rebuild. Not perhaps, not maybe. *Surely.* His love is lavish, not utilitarian and sparse. He does not skimp on beauty. He is rebuilding your life, precious stone by precious stone, and will not allow the destruction of the past to determine your future.

Pray: *Father, my life has been shattered beyond repair, and only You can rebuild it. I ask You to rebuild my hope and my life with precious jewels. May I trust You as the master craftsman whose riches cannot run out. And may I see Your goodness and beauty as I step into the future.*

35: WHEN GOD GIVES YOU A NEW IDENTITY

Nations will see your righteousness, and all kings your glory. You will be called by a new name that the mouth of the LORD will bestow. You will be a crown of glory in the hand of the LORD, a royal diadem in the palm of your God. No longer will you be called Forsaken, nor your land named Desolate; but you will be called Hephzibah, and your land Beulah; for the LORD will take delight in you, and your land will be His bride. —Isaiah 62:2–4

Isaiah gives this prophecy when God's people were acting anything but righteously, but God sees what His people cannot. One day, other nations will see a righteousness that comes from the God they serve, and God will give His people a new name. What a beautiful picture of our new identity in Christ. As the apostle Paul wrote over five hundred years later, if we are in Christ, we are a new creation, the old has gone, the new has come! (See 2 Corinthians 5:17.)

If we are in Christ, we are a new creation, yet we often cling to our old identity. We may still be calling ourselves names that God no longer calls us. In Isaiah's beautiful prophecy, God replaces the name of a people called Forsaken with the name *Hephzibah,* which means "My delight is in her." No longer were his people abandoned but pursued. Their Desolate land becomes *Beulah,* which means "married," speaking to the wholeness and home, love, and security they would find in the Lord.

The Lord does the same in the lives of His daughters today, replacing their old names with new ones that magnify His love and power.

If you've called yourself *afraid,* trust God to free you from your fear, making you *unafraid.*

If you've called yourself *unlovable,* trust that God will overwhelm you with His love and use you to love those fighting the same battle.

If you've called yourself *lonely,* trust that He will meet your needs and make you a beacon of light to those who need a friend.

The names that defined you in the past are no longer your identity. In this world, you may still experience fear, insecurity, and loneliness, but the Lord says they no longer define you! He has declared that your ultimate identity is in Him, and He will redeem those struggles for His glory, making your life a testament to your new name.

Pray: *Father, through Your Son Jesus Christ, You have made me a new creation. In You, I am not forsaken but delighted in! Help me to embrace my new identity and walk in freedom as I follow You.*

36: WHEN YOU'RE WAITING ON GOD

When You did awesome works that we did not expect, You came down, and the mountains trembled at Your presence. From ancient times no one has heard, no ear has perceived, no eye has seen any God besides You, who acts on behalf of those who wait for Him. —Isaiah 64:3–4

Many people, even fellow Christians, may criticize you for waiting on God. We live in a culture that idolizes initiative, and if something hasn't happened in your life—finding the spouse you've prayed for, being freed from depression, getting pregnant, landing a certain job—others may think it's because you're just not doing enough.

Nowhere in Scripture do we find the words, "God helps those who helps themselves." What we *do* find are profound examples of the heartache that can ensue when we don't wait on Him. Though God had promised Abraham and Sarah a child, after years of barrenness, Sarah decided *it was time to do something already* and pressured Abraham to have a child with her maidservant, Hagar. (Read the full account in Genesis 16–18, 21.) When Hagar became pregnant, things got worse, not better, and lasting strife developed between Sarah and Hagar. Although God remained true to His original promise and gave Sarah a biological son, the strife came to a head when Sarah sent Hagar into the desert with her son Ishmael, afraid that he would get part of her son Isaac's inheritance.

All of this could have been avoided had Abraham refused to give in to Sarah's pressure and instead waited on God.

Waiting on God doesn't mean you don't ever act, only that you stay more attuned to the Holy Spirit's voice than to the voices of others. When you do act, it will be in confident faith, not in fear prompted by others' opinions that you're not doing enough. Some may criticize your decision to turn down that job offer or not go on that date, but you will not miss out on God's plan for your life because you didn't give into human pressure. Though others may view you as crazy, God finds that kind of faith beautiful. He will act in His timing and His way, like the prophet Isaiah said, doing "*awesome works that* [you] *did not expect*"!

Pray: *Father, may I not let others' voices compel me to act out of fear. Help me to wait on You in those areas where I feel pressured to act. I trust that You will act on my behalf in Your way and timing.*

37: WHEN THE WORLD IS DARK

He changes the times and seasons; He removes kings and establishes them. He gives wisdom to the wise and knowledge to the discerning. He reveals the deep and hidden things; He knows what lies in darkness, and light dwells with Him. —Daniel 2:21–22

The world is a dark place. We are constantly inundated with real-time updates on tragedies around the world—from wars to human rights violations to violent religious persecution. Witnessing the fruition of evil on such a large scale can be almost too much to bear.

Daniel's prayer brings comfort and perspective when we feel overwhelmed by world problems. Exiled to Babylon and pressed into the service of a pagan king, stripped of his Hebrew name and given one that honored a false god, Daniel was also well acquainted with evil. When King Nebuchadnezzar had a disturbing dream, he vowed to kill all the wise men in his service if no one could interpret it. Daniel prayed to God for wisdom, and God turned Daniel's darkness into light, revealing the meaning of the dream. Overcome with awe, Daniel proclaims that it is God who controls the happenings on earth, not the leaders who think they do. It is God who puts kings in place and who removes them from power. Wisdom comes from God, no one else.

When the world is careening into chaos, remember that God is in control of history. Evil does not have the last word. We will experience this darkness for a little while more, but when Jesus returns, He will banish it forever.

While we wait for Jesus to return, we have a purpose. We are His ambassadors, much like Daniel was God's ambassador to Nebuchadnezzar. God has put you in this time and place for a reason. Jesus is the ultimate Light, but He has commissioned you to be a light that points to Him. (See Matthew 5:14.) Look up from the chaos and set your eyes on Him. Just as He used Daniel, He will use you to shine His light in a dark world.

Pray: *Lord, You are sovereign over history. No world leader and no evil man has the final say. The world is dark, but Your light illuminates the darkness. Empower me to be a light that reflects Your light, that You may be glorified.*

38: WHEN YOU SAY "EVEN IF"

If the God whom we serve exists, then He is able to deliver us from the blazing fiery furnace and from your hand, O king. But ***even if*** *He does not, let it be known to you, O king, that we will not serve your gods or worship the golden statue you have set up.* —Daniel 3:17–18

Nabeel Qureshi, a former Muslim with an outstanding gift for apologetics, was diagnosed with stage four stomach cancer in his early thirties. In videos detailing his journey, he exuded both faith in God's ability to heal and trust in God's goodness even if He didn't. When Nabeel died in 2017 at age thirty-four, he left a legacy of unyielding faith to a watching world.[4]

4. "Seeking Allah, Finding Jesus: The Christian Testimony of Nabeel Qureshi," April 13, 2019, www.youtube.com/watch?v=k0D8Uz4oQck.

Some believers who followed Nabeel's journey may have wrestled with the question of why God hadn't chosen to heal him. His healing would have been a sign of Jesus's power to the Muslim world, and he could have done so much more to advance God's kingdom. It didn't make any sense. When we wonder why God didn't do something even though He could have, the account of Shadrach, Meshach, and Abednego gives us an eternal perspective. Before King Nebuchadnezzar threw them into the furnace for refusing to bow to his golden statue, they proved that their trust in the Lord was not dependent on whether He did things their way. "*Even if*" was their powerful resolution. Even if God didn't save them, they wouldn't bow down to idols.

God *did* save the three young men from the fire, but He didn't heal Nabeel Qureshi. The earthly outcome was different, but the eternal outcome was the same: God was glorified, and Shadrach, Meshach, Abednego, and Nabeel are all experiencing perfect joy in the presence of Jesus. Nabeel's limited human understanding of why things happened the way they did has been stripped away, and now he can see why his earthly story ended differently than theirs.

We don't know what the outcome of our prayers will be, but we do know that whatever happens on earth, we have a bright future ahead of us: eternity in the presence of Jesus. So while we are on earth, let us aspire to a life that says *even if* God doesn't act as we hope, we will trust in Him.

Pray: *Lord, increase my faith in Your goodness. You can heal, but even if You don't, You are kind. You can do miracles, but even if You don't, You are worthy of praise. Open my spiritual eyes that I may see Your goodness that transcends earthly circumstances.*

39: WHEN YOU FEEL ASHAMED

Therefore, behold, I will allure her and lead her to the wilderness, and speak to her tenderly. There I will give back her vineyards and make the Valley of Achor into a gateway of hope. —Hosea 2:14–15

After you've sinned, what is your first instinct? For many of us, it's to hide from God, ashamed and afraid to ask Him for grace. If it's a sin you've succumbed to again and again, it's easy to fear that there are limits to God's grace. But if you are a follower of Jesus, you can trust that His grace *never* runs out.

God gives us a living metaphor of His grace in the account of Hosea and his adulterous wife Gomer. To illustrate His love for His people, God commands Hosea to forgive and pursue his unfaithful wife. The Lord says of His own unfaithful people, *"I will punish her for the days of the Baals when she burned incense to them, when she decked herself with rings and jewelry, and went after her lovers. But Me she forgot. ...* ***Therefore,*** *behold, I will allure her and lead her to the wilderness, and speak to her tenderly. There I will give back her vineyards and make the Valley of Achor into a gateway of hope"* (Hosea 2:13–15).

Most English teachers would circle that "therefore" in red because it seems out of place. They might jot in the margin, "Whenever you see '*therefore,*' it needs to be clear what it's *there for.*" That's the beauty of God's grace. The "*therefore*" wasn't there for anything His people had done. It was simply there for love.

God's words become even more breathtaking when we learn what "*the Valley of Achor*" represents. *Achor* is translated as "trouble," but it's the *why* behind the trouble that points to God's grace so beautifully.

The valley was named after Achan, who rebelled against the Lord and was stoned to death in that very place. (See Joshua 7:25–26.) The Lord proclaimed that He would transform that very place of sin into a gateway of hope. This foreshadows the redemption to come through Christ over seven hundred years later that created a way for us to "*approach the throne of grace with confidence, so that we may receive mercy and find grace to help us in our time of need"* (Hebrews 4:16). When you've sinned, remember that God's lavish grace doesn't run out. Every time you run to Him in repentance, He will transform the dark valley of your failings into a gateway of hope.

Pray: *Jesus, I'm in awe of Your lavish grace. When I am ashamed of what I've done, may I not hide from You, but run into Your arms and repent, confident that Your grace will never run out.*

40: WHEN YOU WANT TO GIVE UP

So let us know—let us ***press on*** *to know the* L*ORD. As surely as the sun rises, He will appear; He will come to us like the rain, like the spring showers that water the earth.* —Hosea 6:3

It's a common plot that has captivated people throughout the ages—two lovers are separated from one another by the forces of evil, yet they will stop at nothing to find each other. We are transfixed by the example of a love that pursues, one that refuses to give up despite seemingly insurmountable barriers.

The Hebrew word for *"press on"* in this passage can also be translated as "to pursue" or "to chase." It is used frequently in the Old Testament to describe the singlemindedness with which God's people pursue their enemies in battle; it is also used to describe the lovingkindness with which God pursues us. (See Psalm 23:6.)

When you are weary, in a spiritually dry season, or experiencing the consequences of your sin, it may feel beyond you to *"press on to know the* L*ORD*." In those times, remember that the story of pursuit that so captivates your heart is a picture of the covenant love God calls you to. This covenant is a promise of God's faithfulness to you and your faithfulness to Him, a vow of love more binding than a marriage. In this passage, Hosea is prophesying to God's covenant people who have broken their vows. God still loves them boundlessly and plans to restore them. Hosea charges God's people to press on to know the Lord even though they have been unfaithful, to repent and determine to participate actively and earnestly in this love story with the confidence that God will not abandon them but will quench their thirst.

When you are exhausted, discouraged, or feeling the effects of sin, look to Jesus Christ, who came to the world like rain on thirsty ground, the Living Water who eternally quenches your deepest thirst. (See John 6:35.) Whatever you're going through, He will revive your heart. As you pursue the Lord, remember that He has pursued you and continues to pursue you. Nothing in all creation can separate you from His love.

Pray: *Lord, thank You for pursuing me with Your covenant love. As You pursue me, may I pursue You with a faithful heart. Revive my thirsty heart as I press on to know You better.*

41: WHEN YOU HAVE TOO MUCH TO DO

He has shown you, O man, what is good. And what does the LORD require of you but to act justly, to love mercy, and to walk humbly with your God?
—Micah 6:8

It's Sunday evening, and the familiar anxiety builds as you think about all you have to do this week. You're juggling deadlines and responsibilities all while taking care of those you love ... and there simply isn't enough time. You go through your mental list once again, hoping you'll magically find a way to create more time and energy. The anxiety goes deeper than just worrying about checking things off your list. There's a question beneath the anxiety that explains the spiraling thoughts, the increasing heart rate: "What if? What if I don't get everything done?"

Your subconscious answer might be, "I'll be a bad employee, mother, student, church member, or friend," or even "I won't please God." We often take the demands of the world and believe that if we don't fulfill them, it means we are a failure as a Christian. It's good to want to please God, but we often put more pressure on ourselves than God does. God doesn't say that if you don't finish your to-do list, there's something wrong with you.

He doesn't measure your success based on productivity, but on your heart's attitude toward Him.

Micah 6:8 strips away the world's external demands and gives us the three things God prioritizes in His followers. Whatever we do, whether big or small in the world's eyes, He tells us to act justly—to do things with integrity, considering how He would have us act. He tells us to love mercy—to show compassion to those in need, even if this means switching around our schedule and being less productive. He tells us to walk with Him humbly—to view others better than ourselves and to stay close to Him.

Are you shouldering burdens that God didn't ask you to? If you are feeling frantic and frazzled over your never-ending checklist, ask the Lord to give you His perspective on your schedule. Ask Him to show you what it means in your current season to act justly, love mercy, and walk humbly with Him. He offers you wisdom, clarity, and rest.

Pray: *Father, I feel overwhelmed by all I have to do, and I have been afraid that if I don't get everything done, I will be a failure in Your eyes. Give me Your perspective on my schedule and show me what is most important for me to do in this busy season. Most importantly, show me how I can walk more closely with You.*

42: WHEN YOU'RE DOUBTING GOD'S FAITHFULNESS

O Lord, I have heard the report of You; I stand in awe, O Lord, of Your deeds. Revive them in these years; make them known in these years. In Your wrath, remember mercy! —Habakkuk 3:2

When you are facing loss, heartache, or destruction, the enemy loves to tell the lie that God has abandoned you. When the enemy's words seem true and you can't see God's faithfulness in the moment, consider the prophet Habakkuk's example of how to reject the lies and embrace the truth. To trust in God's faithfulness in the present, remember God's faithfulness in the past.

When Habakkuk received a prophecy of destruction, he appealed to the Lord's mercy by remembering what He had done in the past, spending the next several verses recounting how God had saved His people. Revived by remembering what the Lord had done, he broke into a proclamation of praise that defied circumstances:

> *Though the fig tree does not bud and no fruit is on the vines, though the olive crop fails and the fields produce no food, though the sheep are cut off from the fold and no cattle are in the stalls, yet I will exult in the Lord; I will rejoice in the God of my salvation!*
>
> (Habakkuk 3:17–18)

Habakkuk could rejoice because he knew how the story would ultimately end based on what He knew of God's character. Habakkuk had much material to draw on from the accounts of God's people that had been passed down from generation to generation. God made Abraham into a great nation, led His people out of Egyptian oppression, and gave them a new home in the promised land, just to name a few of His deeds.

You too can build your faith by collecting true stories from Scripture and other Christians, past and present. Read Genesis and Exodus to see the very accounts that likely strengthened Habakkuk's faith. Listen to biographies of Christian women who have seen God work mightily in impossible situations.[5] Ask friends to share stories of God's faithfulness in their lives. Reflect on your own life and remember how He has acted on your behalf. Armed with evidence of God's faithfulness in the past, you can be confident that God will revive His works in the present and the future.

Pray: *Lord, I want to build my faith in Your faithfulness. Guide me to stories of those who have seen You work mightily and revive those works in my day!*

---

5. A great place to start is the *Velvet Ashes Legacy Podcast*, which shares captivating biographies of Christian women in missions, velvetashes.com.

43: WHEN THE HOLY SPIRIT EMPOWERS YOU

So he said to me, "This is the word of the Lord to Zerubbabel: Not by might nor by power, but by My Spirit, says the Lord of Hosts. What are you, O great mountain? Before Zerubbabel you will become a plain. Then he will bring forth the capstone accompanied by shouts of 'Grace, grace to it!'"
—Zechariah 4:6–7

Sometimes God calls us to a work that is far beyond our ability to show the power of the Holy Spirit and the abundance of His grace. When He does that, He reminds us of the greatest work He has done through His grace, rescuing us from our sin and transforming us into His people.

After God's people had returned from seventy years in Babylonian captivity, it was time to rebuild the temple. Zerubbabel was the man God chose for the job. He and his men completed the temple's foundation in two years, but after that, circumstances caused construction to cease for *almost twenty years*. Through the prophet Zechariah, God encouraged Zerubbabel to continue the project He'd called him to even though it seemed beyond him. God didn't empower Zerubbabel by telling him that he was strong and capable. Instead, He said the Holy's Spirit would equip him to build the temple.

Zerubbabel's story of empowerment by the Holy Spirit points to the greater reality of salvation through Christ. While Zerubbabel had the Holy Spirit helping him rebuild the temple, in Christ, we now *are* the temple where the Holy Spirit lives! (See 1 Corinthians 3:16.) The same Holy Spirit who empowered Zerubbabel to complete a task far too difficult for him is the same Holy Spirit who lives in us. Salvation was far too difficult for us—we were unable to do anything apart from Christ—but through His power and mercy, He saved us.

As the Holy Spirit empowered Zerubbabel to rebuild the temple, the Holy Spirit empowers you to bear the fruit of "*love, joy, peace, patience, kindness, goodness, faithfulness, gentleness, and self-control*" (Galatians 5:22–23), none of which you could produce on your own. Every time you see the Spirit produce godly fruit in your life, let it point you to His greatest work: drawing you to Jesus and experiencing new life with Him.

Pray: *Father, it is not by my might or by my power that I have been saved from my sin, but by Your Spirit! Because of what Jesus has done, the Holy Spirit now lives in me and empowers me to live for You. May I always keep Your power and grace in view.*

44: WHEN YOU'RE TEMPTED

Then the devil took Him to the holy city and set Him on the pinnacle of the temple. "If You are the Son of God," he said, "throw Yourself down. For it is written: 'He will command His angels concerning You, and they will lift You up in their hands, so that You will not strike Your foot against a stone.'" Jesus replied, "It is also written: 'Do not put the Lord your God to the test.'"
—Matthew 4:5–7

Our Savior shows us how to fight temptation: by rightly wielding the Word of God. Three times, the devil tempts Jesus—first, to turn bread into stones to prove His deity; then to throw Himself off the temple roof to provoke angels to rescue Him; and finally to bow down to the devil in exchange for earthly power and glory. To each temptation, Jesus responds, *"It is written,"* shutting the devil down with the truth of God.

We frequently face temptation, and the devil can be very convincing. He has been preying on people for millennia since deceiving Eve into taking his word over God's. But when we know the Word of God, we will recognize a lie when we hear it.

When we don't know the Word very well, we are vulnerable to being deceived by those who twist it. The devil twisted Scripture when he tempted Jesus to throw Himself off the temple roof. Quoting Psalm 91:11–12, the devil said, *"He will command his angels concerning you. … They will lift you up in their hands, so that you will not strike your foot against a stone."* The Word Himself responded to Satan's twisting of Scripture with Deuteronomy 6:16: *"Do not test the Lord your God."*

Let us make it our goal to love, know, and understand God's Word, so that calling the truth to mind may become as natural as breathing. Dig deep into Scripture, not only skimming the surface, but studying God's Word so that you're prepared to respond to deception when it comes. As the apostle Paul says, the Word of God is a weapon, *"the sword of the Spirit"* (Ephesians 6:17). With it, you can pierce the lies of the devil and have victory over sin.

Pray: *Jesus, thank You for Your example in responding to temptation by rightly wielding Your Word. Holy Spirit, guide me as I study the Scriptures, that I may be prepared to recognize deception and overcome temptation when it comes.*

45: WHEN YOU DON'T KNOW WHAT TO PRAY

So then, this is how you should pray: "Our Father in heaven, hallowed be Your name. Your kingdom come, Your will be done, on earth as it is in heaven." —Matthew 6:9–10

When you go to the Lord in prayer, is your mind so overwhelmed by your concerns, needs, and anxieties that you don't know where to start? Jesus teaches us how to begin our prayer time in a way that aligns our hearts with His will and calms our anxiety.

Jesus teaches us to first acknowledge God's relationship to us. Beginning with *"Our Father"* shapes all the prayers that follow. When we acknowledge that He is our Father, we will not pray as though pleading to a far-off deity who has forgotten us, but to One who loves us and gives good gifts to His children. He has invited us into His family, and He is worthy of our honor and obedience.

Jesus teaches us to do one more thing before we make a request—to submit our wills to His. We should pray for His name to be hallowed—to be honored and glorified—for His kingdom to come, and His will to be done. The key word here is *His*. We often come to God with an entitled attitude of *my* will be done. These prayers often reveal that we think we know better than God. When we pray with this attitude, we will remain anxious as we try to convince God to bend to our will. When we trust that God's plan is better than ours and ask for His will to be done, we will experience peace.

Only when we believe that God is a good Father and submit to His will can we relax into our prayers and let go of the plans we have devised. Only when this is our heart posture can we bring our requests to God with open hands, knowing that His will is good.

So before you pray, remember who you're praying to—your Father in heaven. And before you ask for yourself, ask for His will. This is the key to a powerful prayer life filled with joy and hope instead of anxiety and control.

Pray: *Father in heaven, may Your name be glorified. May Your kingdom come and Your will be done in my heart, in my home, in my community, and in the world around me. I submit my will to Yours, confident that Your will is good and kind.*

46: WHEN YOU'RE AFRAID YOU'RE WASTING YOUR LIFE

And if anyone gives even a cup of cold water to one of these little ones because he is My disciple, truly I tell you, he will never lose his reward.
—Matthew 10:42

Have you ever worried that you are not *doing enough* for God? Whether you're a new mom whose days consist of caring for your baby's needs, working a tiresome desk job, or struggling to stay afloat as you battle depression, your daily life may seem small and insignificant. Maybe before this season, you dreamed of doing something *big* for the Lord, something that was measurable and had visible impact.

In the routine or hectic rhythm of your life, you may not have much to measure. Just bits and pieces of fragmented time, sporadic prayers—the anxious inhale and exhale of "Lord, help me" in the hidden spaces of laundry, diapers, piles of bills, and getting out of bed when sadness weighs heavy on your chest. Nothing you do puts you on your imagined trajectory toward hearing the Lord say, *"Well done, good and faithful servant!"* (Matthew 25:21). In your most vulnerable moments, you may wonder if you're wasting your life.

Jesus offers a beautiful truth you can cling to in the mundane: *"And if anyone gives even a cup of cold water to one of these little ones because he is My disciple, truly I tell you, he will never lose his reward"* (Matthew 10:42). When you wake up, bleary eyed and weary, to feed your baby in the middle of the night ... when you are kind to the coworker who has been short-tempered with you ... when you offer hospitality to those struggling when you're struggling too—these are all things that Jesus notices and values.

Your life doesn't need to make it into a bestseller, a superhero movie, or a missionary biography filled with tales of adventure, for if you follow Jesus, your name is written in the *"Book of Life"* (Revelation 21:27). You are being a good and faithful servant when you trust God, follow His commands, and love others. He sees everything you do in His name, and He will reward your hidden faithfulness.

Pray: *Lord, I've believed the lie that I'm wasting my life if I don't do something big for You. Help me to stay faithful in the mundane, hidden things, trusting that You do not measure things as humans do and that everything done in Your name, no matter how small, is precious to You.*

47: WHEN YOU NEED COMPASSION

When He stepped ashore and saw a large crowd, He had compassion on them and healed their sick. —Matthew 14:14

When you are struggling with depression, anxiety, or pain, how do you imagine Jesus? Do you picture Him rolling His eyes, telling you to just snap out of it? Do you picture Him stoic, vacant-eyed, indifferent to the sharpness of your struggle? Many believers think that although Jesus might love them, it's a begrudging love, akin to a husband who resents his wife but sticks with her simply because he made a vow.

But none of that is true. Jesus loves you fiercely and compassionately. Think about a time you were so upset that you couldn't eat—the tangled stomach, the inner groan. This is how Jesus feels when He sees you in pain.

The English word for *compassion* doesn't fully communicate His heart. We may know it means "suffering with," but we rarely use it to describe a heart completely entering into another's grief. The Greek word used for Christ's compassion in Matthew, Mark, and Luke is *splagchnizomai,* which means "bowels," then thought to house the emotions. The literal meaning of the word is "to be moved as to one's bowels," or having a gut-wrenching compassion.

When Jesus saw the crowd drowning in weakness, pain, and hopelessness, He didn't heal out of reluctant obligation to a promise He regretted making. He didn't act so that those He healed would do more for Him. No, instead His stomach turned, and His eyes were filled with love and tears.

Even more remarkable, Jesus showed this intense compassion while grieving the loss of His cousin John, who had just been brutally murdered. If you've ever hesitated to bring your pain to the Lord because you've thought He probably has more important problems to deal with, remember that even in the midst of great personal grief, Jesus didn't turn the crowd away but had compassion on them.

When Jesus sees you suffering, it's as though He were the one in pain. On the days you can't get out of bed, His eyes aren't full of scorn but tears. In every day, every moment, He is moved with gut-wrenching compassion for this child He loves.

Pray: *Father, open my eyes to see Your Son Jesus as He truly is. For every thought that says You are distant and uncaring, replace it with the image of*

Jesus weeping with me. You are greatly moved by my suffering, and I praise You for Your compassion, a compassion that is vastly different from anything the world can offer.

48: WHEN FOLLOWING JESUS IS DIFFICULT

Then Jesus told His disciples, "If anyone wants to come after Me, he must deny himself and take up his cross and follow Me. For whoever wants to save his life will lose it, but whoever loses his life for My sake will find it."
—Matthew 16:24–25

To carry a cross, you have to put everything else down. Holding on to other things is not an option—a cross is heavy and unwieldy, requiring all your strength and attention. Jesus tells His disciples that following Him is difficult. It literally involves denying oneself—one's comforts, one's dreams, one's security—and instead carrying something very heavy along a road that leads toward death.

Jesus promises us, though, that this road toward death is also a path to life. In choosing to lay down human ambition, the pursuit of selfish desires, and a kingdom of self, we get to experience eternal life with Him.

The self-denial Jesus speaks of isn't self-flagellation but submitting yourself to His will. He has put you in this time and place for a purpose, and He will call you to give up things that you wouldn't have to if you weren't His follower. If persecution is rampant where you live, this could mean giving your earthly life. For many of us, though, this means denying our selfish desires and walking as Jesus walked.

When we choose to follow Jesus, our lives will look different than they would have without Him. To the world, we may seem pitiful, as though we are wasting our lives and our talent. The world may question the woman who stays at a low-paying job because she feels called to share the gospel with those particular coworkers. They may scoff at the woman who is getting older and isn't married because she's waiting for a man who also follows Jesus. They may wonder why the young woman with a college degree is serving as a missionary. The world may look on and view us as poor and unloved, but the Christ follower knows better—she is rich, and God loves her fiercely.

Do you need to set anything down so you can take up your cross and follow Jesus with an undivided heart? Are you holding on to worries about finances, relationships, or ambitions that are preventing you from following Him wholeheartedly? Taking up your cross to follow Jesus is difficult, but it is more than worth it. When you take up your cross and follow Him, you will experience life to the fullest, both now and for eternity.

Pray: *Jesus, reveal anything that is preventing me from taking up my cross and give me the courage to lay it down. You are better than anything the world could offer, and I want to follow You with all my heart.*

49: WHEN YOU WONDER IF YOUR PAIN MATTERS

And a woman was there who had suffered from bleeding for twelve years. She had borne much agony under the care of many physicians and had spent all she had, but to no avail. Instead, her condition had only grown worse. When the woman heard about Jesus, she came up through the crowd behind Him and touched His cloak. For she kept saying, "If only I touch His garments, I will be healed." Immediately her bleeding stopped, and she sensed in her body that she was healed of her affliction. —Mark 5:25–29

Have you ever hesitated to go to God because you wonder if your pain matters to Him? Maybe you're comparing yourself to those who seem to have it worse, and you fear that in light of others' struggles, God will view your desperate laments as the complaints of a spoiled child. This fear couldn't be further from the truth. Your cries do not exasperate the Lord; they move Him with compassion. He does not judge pain as humans do, organizing people's struggles into levels of importance.

Jesus was on the way to the house of Jairus, whose sick daughter was moments from death when the woman in Mark 5 touched the hem of

Jesus's garment. She was immediately healed without a word, yet Jesus still stopped and spoke with her, commending her faith. (See Mark 5:34.) From a natural viewpoint, impending death was much more urgent than interacting with a woman who had already been healed. But Jesus is not limited by time and encouraging this newly healed woman mattered to Him even though it wasn't as urgent in the world's eyes.

Before Jesus arrived at Jairus's house, the little girl died. If He hadn't stopped, perhaps He would have gotten there while she was still alive. However, what seemed to be a poor decision brought more glory to God in the long run—He raised the little girl from the dead, showing His power over life and death. Unlike mere men, Jesus did not have to choose whose pain was worse and triage accordingly. His healing was boundless.

Your pain matters to Jesus. Greatly. He is not in a hurry to do more important things, and He does not compare your pain to that of others. Like the woman who touched the hem of His garment, go to Him boldly, and He will meet you there, unhurried and full of compassion.

Pray: *Jesus, thank You for Your boundless compassion. You do not ration Your love or care or compare my pain to that of others, but You comfort me in all my pain. Protect my mind from the enemy's lies, so that I may always run to You in my time of need.*

50: WHEN YOU NEED A FATHER'S LOVE

At once Jesus was aware that power had gone out from Him. Turning to the crowd, He asked, "Who touched My garments?" His disciples answered, "You can see the crowd pressing in on You, and yet You ask, 'Who touched Me?'" But He kept looking around to see who had done this. Then the woman, knowing what had happened to her, came and fell down before Him trembling in fear, and she told Him the whole truth. "Daughter," said Jesus, "your faith has healed you. Go in peace and be free of your affliction." —Mark 5:30–34

The woman with the issue of blood had suffered much more than a physical ailment over the past twelve years. Not only was she weakened by the constant flow of blood, but she was isolated from the community. Constantly unclean according to Jewish law, she had to remain separate and avoid touching others so they wouldn't become unclean. In a way, she may have felt cut off from the family of God. When she touched the hem of Jesus's garment and He faced her, she may have braced herself for harsh words and a command to leave, for she had made this holy man unclean. Instead of chastising her though, Jesus called her *daughter,* a word of family, home, and belonging.

It's interesting that her story interrupts an earthly father's quest to save His own daughter from death. When the woman touched Jesus, He was en route to heal Jairus's dying daughter. In Jairus, we see a good earthly father who would stop at nothing to save his daughter's life. Though he was an imperfect human, his love for his little girl compelled him to do whatever it took for her healing. How much more does our heavenly Father seek to rescue His daughters! Although we see no earthly father advocating for the suffering woman, Jesus's words and actions exude God's fatherly love. Not only did He heal her, He stopped to encourage her, commend her faith, and call her *daughter.*

Whether you have a loving earthly father or not, your Father in heaven loves you just as He loved the suffering woman in Mark 5. When you need a father's love, you have the Father's love. His love is not in a hurry. His love advocates for you when you feel alone in the world. His love calls you *daughter* and invites you into His family, giving you a new name and new life.

Pray: *Father in heaven, thank You for adopting me as Your daughter and for giving me a new identity. Help me to believe in the love You have for me and to embrace my identity as Your daughter.*

51: WHEN YOU'RE STRUGGLING TO BELIEVE

Someone in the crowd replied, "Teacher, I brought You my son, who has a spirit that makes him mute. ... It often throws him into the fire or into the water, trying to kill him. But if You can do anything, have compassion on us and help us." "If You can?" echoed Jesus. "All things are possible to him who believes!" Immediately the boy's father cried out, "I do believe; help my unbelief!" —Mark 9:17, 22–24

The struggle behind many of our struggles is unbelief—unbelief that God sees us, that He is working in our lives, and that His plan is good. Even as Christians, we are still susceptible to the serpent's lie that God is holding out on us. As we wrestle with our unbelief, it feels infuriating; doubts linger when all we want to do is trust God. Maybe we've even had a *mountaintop* experience with God when in the heat of emotion, we declared, "This time, I will no longer waver. I will see God for who He is and never look back."

It would be wonderful if in one moment, we could fully accomplish Hebrews 12:1, to *"throw off every encumbrance and the sin that so easily entangles, and ... run with endurance the race set out for us."* But in our fallen minds in this fallen world, dealing with unbelief is not a one-time, theatrical shedding of a burden, but a daily untangling of all that entangles.

The writer of Hebrews hits on something important. Sin easily entangles us. And from the time of Adam and Eve's sin in the garden, unbelief has been the default setting of our fallen minds. The only way to untangle ourselves from its chains is to look to the truth of God's Word daily, even when our hearts don't respond the way we want.

The man in Mark 9 gives a raw example of how we can boldly come to Jesus with the tension between our belief and unbelief. Instead of turning us away, He will help us to believe. We won't believe perfectly until we see Jesus face to face. We *will* waver many times. This is why we need a Savior, and praise God that we do have a Savior in Jesus Christ!

So when you struggle with unbelief, do not be discouraged; you are in good company. Only look to the Lord, be honest with Him, and trust that He will strengthen your faith and show His faithfulness.

Pray: *Jesus, I do believe that You are good, faithful, and true, but I need You to help the part of me that doesn't believe. Steady my heart and increase my faith.*

52: WHEN GOD CHANGES YOUR PLANS

"I am the Lord's servant," Mary answered. "May it happen to me according to your word." Then the angel left her. —Luke 1:38

Mary probably had a simple, peaceful plan for her life. Marry Joseph, live quietly, and raise lots of children. Imagine the emotions that coursed through her young frame when the angel Gabriel told her that she would become the mother of the long-awaited Messiah! In one swift moment, all her plans dissolved. She could have responded with fear, for the consequences of being pregnant out of wedlock could be grave. She could have responded in anger, upset that her hopes and dreams had been upended. Instead, Mary offered a simple *yes,* calling herself *"the Lord's servant."*

How was Mary able to give such a peaceful, confident *yes* when she learned that God had completely changed her plans? That kind of yes hints at a life of quiet faithfulness. In verse 30, Gabriel told her that she had *"found favor with God."* Mary had likely said yes to the Lord many times before in the small things, and her habit of trust prepared her to embrace God's unexpected plan for her life.

When she said yes, she said yes to a life that would no longer be steady and predictable but would encompass the highest highs and the lowest lows. Still, she surrendered her plans willingly, and God gave her purpose that made those plans pale in comparison. She spent day after day in the presence of Jesus, saw Him fulfill prophecy, watched Him be brutally murdered but then gloriously resurrected. God's plan for her life was far bigger than her own.

We don't know how God may change our plans, but like Mary, we want to be ready to say *yes* to the Lord whatever He calls us to do. In the meantime, may we cultivate a life of quiet obedience and trust in the Lord. The more we say yes to God, the stories of His faithfulness will multiply, and when He does ask us to do something big, we will be able to say with confidence, "I am the Lord's servant. May it happen to me according to Your word."

Pray: *Father God, I want to cultivate a deep faith in the small things that prepares me to say "yes" when You call me to something beyond my ability. Help me to say yes to You in my daily life. Build in me a deep trust in Your faithfulness, and may I be faithful to You whatever You call me to.*

53: WHEN YOU'RE WAITING ON GOD'S PROMISES

Blessed is she who has believed that the Lord's word to her will be fulfilled.
—Luke 1:45

Mary had just received the biggest shock of her life—a visit by the angel Gabriel. He had told her she would bear the Messiah for whom her people had waited for centuries. She, a common Jewish girl, would be the mother of the Christ. Some might have found Gabriel's promise unbelievable but Mary believed. When she rushed to her cousin Elizabeth, who was in the middle of her own miracle pregnancy, Elizabeth pronounced a blessing over Mary for believing in God's promise.

This blessing can apply to us as well. The Lord has also promised us beautiful things beyond our comprehension. Don't some of God's promises seem too big, too vast, too good to be true? For those who have trusted in Jesus, He has promised eternal life and a future unmarred by tears, pain, or suffering. (See Revelation 21:4.) He has promised us that the suffering we experience on earth won't compare with *"the glory that will be revealed"* when we see Jesus face to face (Romans 8:18).

In the waiting, where we have the promise but have not seen its fulfillment, it is easy to doubt. We may be tempted to lean on the world's wisdom,

wisdom that says this life is all there is, so we'd better look for fulfillment here rather than putting our hope in an outrageous promise. Gabriel's words to Mary stop worldly wisdom in its tracks: *"No word from God will ever fail"* (Luke 1:37). Mary took God at His word, and Gabriel's words proved true. Everything he told her came to pass. The same is true for you.

You too must choose whether you will take God at His word. Dare to follow the example of Mary, who said yes to believing in God's promise to her and was not disappointed. You will not be disappointed either when you fully lean on God's promises. Gabriel's words to Mary are just as true for you: *"No word from God will ever fail."* And as you wait, blessed are you when you believe that the Lord's promises will be fulfilled.

Pray: *Father, sometimes Your promises seem too good to be true, and I doubt. As I read Your Word and read of Your faithfulness, build my trust in Your promises and give me an eternal perspective that waits patiently for their fulfillment.*

54: WHEN YOU'RE PERSECUTED FOR YOUR FAITH

Blessed are you when people hate you, and when they exclude you and insult you and reject your name as evil because of the Son of Man. Rejoice in that day and leap for joy, because great is your reward in heaven. For their fathers treated the prophets in the same way. —Luke 6:22–23

When we think of persecution, we often think of physical violence, but Jesus shares another type of persecution—being insulted and accused of evil because of Him. When your actions stem from the desire to show Christ's love to others, it brings a unique kind of pain. The very love you want the world to see is distorted by the enemy's lies, and instead of coming closer to the beauty and redemption of Christ, others insult you and exclude you.

There are two common responses to this we should avoid. The first is to bend to the world's definition of love. When others view our actions as unloving, we may wrongly believe that to show the love of Christ, we must accept their philosophy as valid. In bending to the world's definition of love though, we lie to others about what God desires, which is anything but loving.

Another response is to give up on sharing Jesus's love with others. You may become angry and adopt an *us versus them* mentality. "If they're going to treat me like that," you think, "then I'll give it right back." Alternatively, you might retreat into your own "Christian bubble," neglecting the mission of sharing Jesus with a dying world.

Jesus offers us a third response: rejoice! Rejoice when we are accused of being evil. Rejoice because He is preparing a reward in heaven for our faithfulness. Rejoice because we are in good company, walking the narrow path with the prophets of old who also were wrongfully accused.

The next time you're accused of evil because of your commitment to Jesus, pay attention to your immediate response. Are you tempted to compromise your convictions? Do you consider lashing out or withdrawing? In that moment, choose to rejoice. Although you may be rejected on earth, you are accepted eternally by your Savior. Though you may not be rewarded for your faith here, He is preparing a reward for you in heaven. Though you may be accused of being evil by those around you, look forward to the day when Jesus invites you into His presence and says, *"Well done, good and faithful servant!"* (Matthew 25:21).

Pray: *Lord Jesus, You say that I am blessed when people call me evil because of Your name. Help me to rejoice in persecution and be faithful when I am insulted, rejected, and hated.*

55: WHEN YOU'RE NOT PERSECUTED FOR YOUR FAITH

Then Jesus said to all of them, "If anyone wants to come after Me, he must deny himself and take up his cross daily and follow Me. For whoever wants to save his life will lose it, but whoever loses his life for My sake will save it." —Luke 9:23

In *The Brothers Karamazov*, a respected monk named Zosima observes that dying to yourself daily can be harder than dying a martyr's death:

> Active love is a harsh and fearful thing compared with love in dreams. Love in dreams thirsts for immediate action, quickly performed, and with everyone watching. Indeed, it will go as far as the giving even of one's life, provided it does not take long but is soon over, as on stage, and everyone is looking on and praising. Whereas active love is labor and perseverance, and for some people, perhaps, a whole science. But I predict that even in that very moment when you see with horror that despite all your efforts, you not only have not come nearer your goal but seem to have gotten farther from it, at that very moment—I predict this to you—you will suddenly reach your goal and will clearly behold over you the wonder-working power of the Lord, who all the while has been loving you, and all the while has been mysteriously guiding you.[6]

Many of us may romanticize the martyr's death and feel that we are lesser Christians if we don't face violent persecution. But Zosima reminds us that loving Christ is about much more than giving one's life in a single moment; it is the arduous daily labor and perseverance of taking up our cross.

When Jesus told the disciples that they must take up their cross daily to follow Him, the cross wasn't yet a victorious symbol. He spoke these words before His death and resurrection, so all the disciples knew was that death on the cross was the most shameful of deaths. Yet Jesus chose this death as a metaphor for the daily cost of following Him. They had to know that in choosing to follow Him, they were signing up to endure steady suffering for His sake.

You may not face martyrdom, but you do have a daily cross to bear. It might be loving a difficult person, enduring chronic pain, or remaining

---

6. Fyodor Dostoevsky, *The Brothers Karamazov*, trans. Richard Pevear and Larissa Volokhonsky (New York: Farrah, Straus and Giroux, 1990), 58.

single because there are no godly men in sight. Whatever cross you bear, you can be confident that the active love you show for Jesus is precious in His sight.

Pray: *Jesus, I have sometimes felt guilty when I compare my life to Christians who are violently persecuted. Help me to view things from Your perspective, knowing that You put me in this time and place for a reason, and I can be a faithful follower by taking up my cross daily and following You.*

56: WHEN YOU'RE STRIVING TO "DO" FOR THE LORD

She had a sister named Mary, who sat at the Lord's feet listening to His message. But Martha was distracted by all the preparations to be made. She came to Jesus and said, "Lord, do You not care that my sister has left me to serve alone? Tell her to help me!" "Martha, Martha," the Lord replied, "you are worried and upset about many things. But only one thing is necessary. Mary has chosen the good portion, and it will not be taken away from her."
—Luke 10:39–41

Martha's heart was noble—the long-awaited Messiah was in her home, and she wanted to serve Him. If there was ever a time to rush around, it was now! When she saw Mary learning at Jesus's feet instead of helping her prepare a meal, she may have questioned her sister's devotion to Him. After all, wasn't *doing* the most valuable way to show your love? Jesus gently broadened Martha's vision, for though her motives were pure, she was missing out on the beautiful gift Jesus offered her. Mary had grasped a precious truth Jesus wanted Martha to understand: God's work *in* her was just as valuable as His work *through* her.

Many of us approach our relationship to Jesus like Martha did, viewing it solely in terms of the measurable value we can bring to His kingdom. Our logic is often faulty: We strive to work for the Lord so that others might be drawn into deep relationship with Jesus, but we don't think we have the privilege of resting in that relationship ourselves. We view God as our employer rather than as our Father.

Like Martha, though our motives may be good, we are missing out on the fullness of what Jesus offers. God works in the hidden places of our hearts when we read His Word, when we wrestle in prayer, when we sit still before Him with no checklist or agenda. This is the *"good portion"* that Jesus describes. Our God is not a utilitarian God. He is the God who leaves the ninety-nine sheep to find the missing one, and when He finds it, He feeds and cares for it.

You are not His distant employee, but His beloved daughter. God's work *in* you is just as valuable as His work *through* you. Receive the good portion that Jesus offers you and embrace the joy of sitting in His presence and watching Him transform you from the inside out.

Pray: *Jesus, teach me to sit at Your feet and learn from You like Mary. Help me to embrace my identity as Your beloved daughter. Broaden my vision and deepen my understanding that I may experience the fullness of relationship with You.*

57: WHEN YOU DON'T HAVE MUCH TO GIVE

Jesus looked up and saw the rich putting their gifts into the treasury, and He saw a poor widow put in two small copper coins. "Truly I tell you," He said, "this poor widow has put in more than all the others. For they all contributed out of their surplus, but she out of her poverty has put in all she had to live on." —Luke 21:1–4

God's economy is different than man's. He doesn't measure our giving by the dollar but by the heart. He doesn't measure our commitment by what we can produce but by the love behind what we do.

Have you ever compared what you can give to what others can? Maybe you have small children, and every moment is spent caring for them. You may compare yourself to the single woman who has a thriving ministry at your local church. Maybe you're that same single woman who is pouring herself into ministry, but you feel it holds less value than discipling children of your own. Perhaps you're in a mental health crisis, and you have nothing to give except desperate prayers. Or perhaps, like the poor widow, you want to give generously but you're struggling financially.

You may be comparing what you can give to what others can, but *Jesus does not.* He doesn't call you to compare your gifts to others but wants you to give generously *according to your ability.* Though it may seem miniscule in the world's eyes, any gift to Jesus is beautiful in His sight when it comes from a heart committed to Him. Giving out of your poverty of spirit—offering another prayer when you are depressed—is as precious as the widow's offering. Getting up to feed your baby in the middle of the night is beautiful to the Lord. Serving your local church once a week when work is busy and your schedule is full is an offering God cherishes.

Turn your eyes from the offerings of others and set them on Jesus. Ask what He wants you to give and what He has called you to in this season, and like the poor widow, give that sacrifice willingly, trusting that the Lord values an offering that comes from the heart.

Pray: *Lord, I don't have much to give, but what I do have, I offer to You. May I not compare my gifts to others, but keep my eyes fixed on You. May I glorify You by giving the very best of what I have.*

58: WHEN YOUR HEART IS LOST IN TRANSLATION

The Word became flesh and made His dwelling among us. We have seen His glory, the glory of the one and only Son from the Father, full of grace and truth. —John 1:14

When you go to a foreign country, even when you know the language, much is often lost in translation. The nuances and intricacies of your native tongue are sanded away until only the general message remains, and you have a hard time fully communicating your heart to those listening.

When the Father spoke to us through Jesus, nothing of His heart was lost in translation. Through Jesus's incarnation, God translated His love in the most powerful and accurate way possible. He spoke our exact language by sending His Son to not only speak words we could understand but to live what we lived. In this divine translation is the intimacy we long for; when He speaks words of truth, He speaks with a deep understanding of our human weakness because He has lived it.

He could have chosen a more efficient way to translate His love, but He chose to trade speed for nuance and numbers for intimacy by growing up in obscurity, thirty years of humility in mundane labor, living an unseen life so similar to ours. Then, in His ministry, again and again, He slowed and stopped to listen to the individual, embracing their story with compassion.

God's people awaited this divine translation for millennia, and we are among those privileged to have access to Him! Hebrews 1:1–2 says, *"On many past occasions and in many different ways, God spoke to our fathers through the prophets. But in these last days* ***He has spoken to us by His Son****, whom He appointed heir of all things, and through whom He made the universe."* God's message through Jesus Christ is unmatched not only because He became flesh but because Jesus is the Creator—He knows how to speak to each heart because He spoke our hearts to life in the first place.

If you ever doubt God's love for you, remember the lengths God went to so you could understand and experience His love. Stand in awe of the Word becoming flesh and worship the God who would stop at nothing to save you.

Pray: *Jesus, thank You for becoming human so that You could show the extent of Your love. You have lived what I have lived, and You fully understand my cares and weaknesses. Help me to believe in Your love and honor You with my life.*

59: WHEN YOU FEEL UNLOVED

For God so loved the world that He gave His one and only Son, that everyone who believes in Him shall not perish but have eternal life. —John 3:16

Four hundred years before Jesus walked the earth, the prophet Malachi records a chilling exchange between God and His people:

> *"I have loved you," says the LORD. But you ask, "How have You loved us?"* (Malachi 1:2)

God's people doubted His love, even after centuries of displaying His faithfulness in the past and His plan to send Jesus prophesied for the future. We often do the same. When we face trials, in our limited perspective, we may also rage at the Lord, cynically shouting, "How have You loved me?" when He doesn't answer our prayers the way we hoped. When we read Scripture about God's love, we may discount it because it doesn't feel true for us, so we push away the words of God's love.

When you doubt God's love, consider this. Jesus answers the question, "How have You loved me?" in today's verse, one of the most famous passages in the Bible: *"For God so loved the world that He gave His one and only Son, that everyone who believes in Him shall not perish but have eternal life."*

In John 3:16, *"so"* means *in this way*. When we ask, "How have You loved us?" God tells us He has loved us *in this way*: He created a rescue plan, one that would require Him to sacrifice His very own Son. He does not want you to die but to live and to live with Him eternally. Later, in John 15:13, Jesus says, *"Greater love has no one than this, that he lay down his life for his friends."* How has He loved us? With the greatest love.

You may not feel His love in the moment, and you may go through times of doubt. But when your heart deceives you, come back to this anchor in Scripture, these words of Jesus's that have resonated throughout millennia. They are just as true for you as they were the moment Jesus spoke them. You can trust in His love for you, a love that wouldn't let anything, even death, stop Him from making a way for you to be reconciled to Him.

Pray: *Father, I have doubted Your love for me. Help me to understand on a deeper level the great love You have for me, demonstrated in the death of Your Son, Jesus Christ.*

60: WHEN YOU SEE JESUS FACE TO FACE

The woman said, "I know that Messiah" (called Christ) "is coming. When He comes, He will explain everything to us." Jesus answered, "I who speak to you am He." —John 4:25–26

Have you imagined what it will be like when you meet Jesus face to face? Jesus's conversation with the Samaritan woman at the well gives us a glimpse of the joy that will eclipse our pain and our questions when we finally come into His presence.

Having had five husbands and now living with a man she wasn't married to, this woman likely struggled with shame and isolation. She came to draw water during the hottest part of the day, presumably so she wouldn't run into any of the respectable women in town. She was also a woman of faith, confident that the coming Messiah would reveal the answers to the questions that God's worshippers had carried for millennia. She was a woman just like us, broken and longing; the only answer to the questions of her heart could not be found in an ordinary man, in works, or in community, but in the Messiah, Jesus.

When Jesus revealed who He was, her countenance and life were transformed. The pain, the loneliness, and the shame were eclipsed in that moment she came face to face with the long-awaited Messiah. The answer to all her questions was *Him*. Overcome with joy, she left her water jar where it was, ran to the city, and told everyone about Jesus.

You may feel as broken as the woman at the well, seeking to understand the painful questions and mysteries of this life. Although Jesus has been revealed to us, we still live in a broken world, and though we know the truth, we don't always feel it. One day, we will feel the truth as clearly as we know it. If you are a follower of Jesus, you can look forward to your own face-to-face encounter with the Messiah, when all your questions will be answered in Him. The mystery and questions that plagued you on earth will dissolve, replaced by the joyful clarity of Jesus's presence. The best is yet to come.

Pray: *Jesus, I can't wait for the day when I see You face to face. Thank You for revealing Yourself to me, for saving me from my sins, for giving me hope and an eternal future with You. During my days on earth, may I trust that one day, my faith will become sight, and the sight of You will answer every question, every heartbreak, and every longing.*

61: WHEN JESUS DOESN'T SEEM LIKE ENOUGH

Jesus answered, "I am the bread of life. Whoever comes to Me will never hunger, and whoever believes in Me will never thirst." —John 6:35

Have you ever asked yourself, "If Jesus is the bread of life, then why do I feel so hungry?" As a follower of Jesus, you may imagine something is wrong with you if you desire other things even though you have the most important thing—a relationship with God. You might think that if Jesus truly were the bread of life, every morning, you would awaken filled with strength and purpose. The earthly desires you used to have would be a speck receding in your rearview mirror as you sped toward Jesus with giddy joy. You would feel the Father's love so deeply that you would never crave human love. You would constantly worship alongside the psalmist, *"As the deer pants for streams of water, so my soul longs after You, O God"* (Psalm 42:1).

For most of us, this isn't the case. We feel hungry, we hurt, we suffer, and then we read a verse like John 6:35 and think there's either something wrong with us ... or with God. Considering a rare genetic disorder may help to reframe the seeming paradox of our hunger and Jesus's words.

Due to a flaw in their fifteenth chromosome, someone suffering from Prader-Willi syndrome (PWS) is constantly plagued by hunger regardless of how much they eat.

As believers, Jesus has promised us an eternally fulfilling future with Him, but until we die or He returns, we must live in a world rife with sin, disease, and heartbreak. Jesus has filled us, but in our disordered world, like someone with PWS, we often are unable to recognize that we are full.

We will grow in being satisfied in Christ on earth, but we won't realize just how full we are until He raises us up on the last day. (See John 6:39.)

Pray: *Jesus, You are the bread of life. I believe that Your Word is true, even when I can't feel it. This world is filled with unfulfilled longings, and I feel so hungry. Help me to hold fast to You and the truth, knowing that one day, I will not only know but experience that You are the bread of life.*

62: WHEN YOU DON'T UNDERSTAND WHY

Now Jesus loved Martha and her sister and Lazarus. So on hearing that Lazarus was sick, He stayed where He was for two days. —John 11:5–6

Jesus's actions made no sense. When Mary and Martha sent word that their brother was sick, Jesus stayed where He was, allowing Lazarus to suffer, painfully decline, and die, all when Jesus could have healed him immediately. John 11:5 tells us that Jesus loved Mary, Martha, and Lazarus, but His inaction seemed anything but loving. By human logic, love would rush to Lazarus's side and heal him.

Jesus's response is illogical from a human standpoint, but He truly did stay away because of His great love for His friends. In fact, He had a plan that far outweighed the healing the sisters asked for. They wanted Lazarus to get well, but He planned to show His power over death. Such an act would also cause those who knew Lazarus to believe and word about Jesus to spread like wildfire.

When Jesus finally arrived two days later, Mary and Martha wrestled with *why* Jesus had stayed away, both saying, *"Lord, if You had been here, my brother would not have died"* (John 11:21, 32). His actions seemed callous, cruel even, withholding good from those He claimed to love. We are often in Mary and Martha's shoes, not understanding why God allowed tragedy to strike or hasn't answered a prayer we've prayed for decades. Our natural response is to lean on our own understanding rather than trusting that God has a greater plan than ours.

Mary and Martha were soon blown away by their brother's resurrection. The timing, which had once seemed so cruel, was impeccable. Because of Jesus's timing, not only were the sisters and Lazarus blessed, but *"many … believed in Him"* (John 11:45). Many Jews had come to comfort Mary and Martha in their grief, and Jesus performed the miracle before their eyes, showing His power over death so that others might believe and be saved. This, dear sister, is the God we serve, the God whose plan is good, whose timing is perfect, and who has a purpose in all He does.

Pray: *Jesus, I don't understand why You have allowed things to turn out the way they have. Help me to trust that Your plan is better than mine and that You have a purpose in all You do. Help me not to lean on my understanding, but on Your goodness.*

63: WHEN YOU'RE GRIEVING

"Jesus wept." —John 11:35

Your pain matters to Jesus.

Whatever you're grieving, however big or small in the world's eyes, your pain matters to Him. He doesn't compare or measure grief like humans do. He is not utilitarian or mathematical in His approach. No, He is a present, constant friend who will weep with you.

When Jesus wept with Mary and Martha after their brother Lazarus died, He knew that in a matter of minutes, their grief would be turned to joy, that their tears would be momentary and pale in comparison to the coming miracle. Even with that knowledge, He didn't shame Mary or Martha for their lack of faith. He didn't compare their pain to others', telling them that many had it worse than they did. He didn't tell them to look on the bright side. Before the miracle, before He turned their grief to joy, He wept as though Mary and Martha's finite eyes were His.

When you are grieving, you can weep before Him with no fear of judgment. As His follower, you may know that your "*light and momentary affliction is producing for* [you] *an eternal glory that is far beyond comparison*" (2 Corinthians 4:17) but it often doesn't feel that way. It was much the same for Martha. She expressed faith in Jesus that her brother would be raised one day in the final resurrection, but nonetheless, her heart was wracked with pain in the present. Jesus understood Martha's pain. He walked the earth as a human too and understands that grief in the present often outshouts hope for the future. When you go to Christ for comfort, just as He wept with Martha, He will weep with you.

When you are grieving, run to the Lord like Martha ran to Him, confident that though He knows the beautiful future you have ahead, He feels every ounce of your pain in the present. He will be near to you and will comfort you. Your pain matters to Him.

Pray: *Jesus, You are the same God today as You were when You grieved with Mary and Martha. Thank You for comforting me in my grief, for weeping with me when I can't imagine that anything good can come out of my pain. You see the beginning from the end, yet You choose to grieve with me in the present. Thank You for your kindness and closeness.*

64: WHEN OTHERS DON'T UNDERSTAND YOUR CALLING

Then Mary took about a pint of expensive perfume, made of pure nard, and she anointed Jesus' feet and wiped them with her hair. And the house was filled with the fragrance of the perfume. —John 12:3

Can you imagine spending an entire year's wages on perfume, only to immediately pour it on the ground? This is exactly what Mary of Bethany did, pouring a bottle of precious nard on Jesus's feet. Judas Iscariot jumped in with judgment, saying that the nard could have been sold and the money given to the poor. We don't know what the others were thinking, but awkward silence may have followed, an unspoken, "What a waste" hanging in the air.

We may also face times when God calls us to do something that others see as a waste. They may see your actions as an unwise use of time, money, or youth, but if God has called you to it, His voice is the only one that matters. It is wise to get godly advice, but people are no substitute for the Holy Spirit. Don't allow fear of what others will think to stop you from taking the step of faith God is calling you to. If others think you're crazy, you're in good company. Along with Mary of Bethany, we see Noah building an ark while those around him likely thought he had gone insane. We see the prophets proclaiming God's Word while God's people mocked and rejected them. We see Jesus's disciples leaving everything to follow Him. And we see Jesus Himself, who came not as the warrior-savior His people expected, but as a humble teacher executed on a Roman cross. What a waste, right? No! All of these people were willing to look crazy to the world out of their commitment to God's will, and each story ended with God being glorified.

If God calls you to something that seems foolish in the world's eyes, call to mind Jesus's defense of Mary's unorthodox actions. He didn't agree with Judas but told him, *"Leave her alone"* (John 12:7). Jesus is the only one you need to please, and when you seek to please Him, your costly acts of faith are not wasteful but beautiful.

Pray: *Father, may I only look to You for approval in all I do. Help me to be faithful to do what You call me to do, no matter how strange or extravagant it looks to others. Guide my steps and my actions in a way that is beautiful to You.*

65: WHEN A DREAM HAS DIED

But Jesus replied, "The hour has come for the Son of Man to be glorified. Truly, truly, I tell you, unless a kernel of wheat falls to the ground and dies, it remains only a seed; but if it dies, it bears much fruit. Whoever loves his life will lose it, but whoever hates his life in this world will keep it for eternal life." —John 12:23–25

Are you grieving a dream that has died? One you anticipated for years and saw come true for many, but not for you? You wrestled with God in prayer like Jacob, hoped against all hope like Abraham, yet now, it is clear that the dream has died.

During those days of wrestling in prayer, you clung to the accounts of Hannah, who received the child she longed for, and Lazarus, who was raised from the dead. It was easy to put your hope in those Scriptures more than putting hope in Jesus Himself. It was also easy to put your hope in the well-meaning voices of friends and family who said that if God placed a dream in your heart, He would certainly fulfill it.

But in John 12:24, we see Jesus preparing not just for the death of a dream, but for the ultimate death. He dreaded it but knew that it would bring life to the world. We are to follow Jesus in the same way, trusting that the suffering and mourning of the dream He didn't fulfill are *"producing for us an eternal glory that is far beyond comparison"* (2 Corinthians 4:17). Our hope is not in the fulfillment of our earthly dreams, but in Christ Himself.

That dead dream can be a kernel of wheat that reflects Jesus, a death that will bring life. If you could see all that He is doing as you surrender that dream, you would stand in awe. You can still grieve the dream—Jesus Himself sweat blood before His death—but you don't have to die with it. He who raised you from death to life, who has made you a new creation, works everything for your good, and when you get to the end of your life and look back, you will see beyond a shadow of a doubt that following Him was worth it.

Pray: *Jesus, I am grieving a dream I've had for so long, but I know it is time to let go. Please comfort me and teach me to put my hope in You whatever comes in this life. May this kernel of wheat that has fallen to the ground bear much fruit.*

66: WHEN IT SEEMS LIKE GOD ISN'T WORKING

"Woman, why are you weeping?" Jesus asked. "Whom are you seeking?" Thinking He was the gardener, she said, "Sir, if you have carried Him off, tell me where you have put Him, and I will get Him." Jesus said to her, "Mary." She turned and said to Him in Hebrew, "Rabboni!" (which means "Teacher"). —John 20:15–16

Mary Magdalene's hopes and dreams had unraveled before her eyes. After her life was dramatically changed by Jesus, she left everything to follow Him. She was sure He was the Messiah, the One who was to save her people, yet she had witnessed His brutal crucifixion with her own eyes. Wracked with grief, she went to Jesus's grave three days later to see that the stone had been rolled away. It appeared that His body had been stolen and His tomb desecrated.

This faithful woman wept, her heart now a question mark, perhaps wondering what God was doing or if all she'd believed was a lie. Through her tears, she couldn't see that the man standing before her was the very One she was grieving. When it looked like all was lost, the miracle had already taken place, and its proof was now before her, calling her by name.

"Mary," Jesus said, the sound of her name on His lips making the scales fall from her eyes. He had been there all along. Her faith became sight, and her sorrow melted into giddy joy.

Are we not like Mary before Jesus called her name, wrongly interpreting the work of God through eyes blurred by the tears of earthly grief? How often do we question whether He's working, whether our faith has been in vain, only to have Him right there beside us, calling us by name. In our blurry present, we have the privilege of looking at the clarity of the past, of the truth revealed to His servant Mary, the first in a long line of women who tasted what it meant to follow Jesus and never turned back. One day, our faith too will become sight, but for now, we can trust from the evidence of the past that our God is working, and that the same God who called Mary by name calls your name as well.

Pray: *Father, I don't see what You are doing and all hope seems lost, but just as You revealed Yourself to Mary, my faith will one day become sight. In the mystery, in the waiting, may I trust that You are working out a good plan.*

67: WHEN YOU'RE COMPARING YOUR LIFE WITH OTHERS'

"Truly, truly, I tell you, when you were young, you dressed yourself and walked where you wanted; but when you are old, you will stretch out your hands, and someone else will dress you and lead you where you do not want to go." Jesus said this to indicate the kind of death by which Peter would glorify God. And after He had said this, He told him, "Follow Me." … When Peter saw [John], he asked, "Lord, what about him?" Jesus answered, "If I want him to remain until I return, what is that to you? You follow Me!"
—John 21:18–19, 21–22

Peter had just received heavy news from Jesus—he would be martyred for his faith. Interestingly, Peter's first response was to look at the apostle John and ask Jesus, *"Lord, what about him?"* When Peter asked that question, he did something that we do all too often, comparing God's plan for his life to God's plan for someone else's life.

We often compare others' blessings to our sorrows. When we see the woman announcing her pregnancy after years of our own painful infertility, we may ask God, "Why her but not me?" When our friend gets a promotion while we struggle to make ends meet, we may ask God, "Why haven't You provided for me in the same way?" Jesus's response to Peter shows us that knowing the *why* doesn't matter; what matters is following Him on the path He has for our life.

Whenever we compare, we shift our eyes from Jesus onto ourselves. He has marked out a unique plan for each of us, paved with joys and hardships different from others'. When you are comparing your sorrows to another woman's blessings, when you cry out to understand why He hasn't given you the same path as hers, remember Jesus's words to Peter, *"What is that to you? You follow Me!"*

Jesus's words sound harsh, but they come from love because when we ask *why*, we're asking the wrong question. The right question is *who?* Our ultimate calling isn't to compare experiences, to rate joys and sorrows and answered prayers, but to follow Jesus, whatever that looks like. One day, we may understand the *why*, but for now, what is that to us? Let's focus on the *who* and follow wherever He leads.

Pray: *Lord, I often compare the life You've given me to the life You've given to other women, and I have taken my eyes off You. Help me to keep my eyes firmly set on You and the path You have for my life.*

68: WHEN YOU'RE SEEKING THE GIFT OVER THE GIVER

Men, why are you doing this? We too are only men, human like you. We are bringing you good news that you should turn from these worthless things to the living God, who made heaven and earth and sea and everything in them. In past generations, He let all nations go their own way. Yet He has not left Himself without testimony to His goodness: He gives you rain from heaven and fruitful seasons, filling your hearts with food and gladness.
—Acts 14:15–17

When Paul healed a lame man in Lystra, chaos ensued. Amazed by the healing, the people immediately started worshipping Paul and his fellow missionary Barnabas, calling them Hermes and Zeus. Horrified, Paul explained that they were not gods, and it was God's power that healed the man, not theirs. They explained that God's gifts point to Him but are not the ultimate things in and of themselves.

At first glance, we may not think we have much in common with the Lycaonians, but we too are tempted to worship the conduits of God's grace more than God Himself.

Instead of worshipping God, the people worshipped Paul and Barnabus. Have you ever found yourself worshipping a person? Perhaps you worship what your parents think of you, and you feel you will only be acceptable if you have their acceptance. Perhaps you worship your image of a godly spouse, and undergirding your prayers for a godly husband is the belief that a man can meet your needs better than God can.

Paul also lists material things God provides for our enjoyment, but these are gifts, not the ultimate goal. When you pray for God to provide, do you secretly believe that if you just had more money, you would feel secure? Though God does provide materially for His children, we miss the most important thing when we worship people and provision rather than the Provider, when we rush past the embrace of the Giver to greedily open His gifts.

When you find yourself pursuing God's gifts rather than pursuing Him, ask yourself Paul's simple question to the people of Lystra, "*Why are you doing this?*" God Himself is far greater than His gifts, and when we understand this, we will experience peace and joy where there has been fear and striving. If you have been clinging to His gifts rather than to Him, unclench your fists, trusting that He is more than enough to satisfy your needs.

Pray: *Father, I have pursued Your gifts more than I have pursued You. My mind knows You are greater than Your gifts, but my heart often deceives me. Teach me to worship You and You alone.*

69: WHEN IT'S DIFFICULT TO PRAY

In the same way, the Spirit helps us in our weakness. For we do not know how we ought to pray, but the Spirit Himself intercedes for us with groans too deep for words. And He who searches our hearts knows the mind of the Spirit, because the Spirit intercedes for the saints according to the will of God.
—Romans 8:26–27

Imagine being wrongfully arrested in a foreign country where you only know a few words of the language. Even if you could express your innocence, you don't have any knowledge of the nation's legal processes and how to make a case for yourself. The situation seems hopeless, until the country's most renowned lawyer decides to be your advocate. He not only translates your plight to the judge but articulates it with beauty and persuasion. This is how the Holy Spirit intercedes for us when we don't know what to pray.

When we're suffering, prayer can feel impossible. In our mental anguish, the pain runs so deep, there is no human language that can express our desperation. As those who are indwelt by the Holy Spirit, though, we can take heart. The Holy Spirit intercedes for us to the Father, persuasively articulating exactly what we need according to God's will.

These prayers from the Holy Spirit to the Father's ears are the most intimate and powerful that can occur—the profound mystery of the Godhead is that they are One and share the same will. The Father always answers prayers within His will, so you can be assured that the Spirit's groans on your behalf will be answered.

God's solutions, healing, and rescue are often a direct result of the Holy Spirit's praying on our behalf. He knows exactly what we need and intervenes in ways we would never have thought to pray for.

At this very moment, the Holy Spirit is pleading before the Father for you with groans that human language cannot express, and the Father is responding with the tender love that defines Him. He will answer, and He will surprise you with the brilliance and intricacy of His plan for your life.

Pray: *Holy Spirit, I don't have the words to pray. I thank You knowing that at this very moment, You are articulating exactly what I need to the Father. May I rest in You as You intercede on my behalf.*

70: WHEN YOUR MIND NEEDS RENEWAL

Do not be conformed to this world, but be transformed by the renewing of your mind. Then you will be able to test and approve what is the good, pleasing, and perfect will of God. —Romans 12:2

Do you ever think about the same things today that you pondered yesterday? Rumination or repetitive thinking can be a problem when we dwell on things that make us feel anxious or worried about the future, upset about something in the past, or missing out on something today.

If we don't take an active role in our thought life, many of our thoughts will conform to those of the surrounding culture. As you consider your inner monologue, can you identify any repetitive thoughts that conform to the world's ideas? Perhaps they are self-disparaging thoughts prompted by marketers trying to convince you that your life will be better if you buy their products. Perhaps social media is filling your mind with vitriol toward the opposite sex, encouraging you to think of all men as bad. Perhaps your workplace is a hotbed of grumbling and complaining, and your thoughts toward your job have becoming increasingly cynical.

We can't remove ourselves from the world, nor should we, but we must be proactive in this process of renewing our minds. First, we must identify *where* we are conforming. Then, we must remove the sources of those thoughts and replace them with the truth of God's Word. This might mean taking a break from social media or turning off the news and spending time in Scripture instead.

As you consider the thoughts that occur to you over and over again, where does your mind need to be renewed? The Lord has given you the gift of His Word so that you can replace the world's messages with His. The world's words bring anxiety, but His words bring peace. The world's words focus on self, but His words point to Christ. The world's words can make you think that life is meaningless, but the Lord's words renew your mind, leading you to His good, pleasing, and perfect will.

Pray: *Father, my mind needs renewing, and I want to exchange the sadness and futility of my worldly thoughts for the joy and hope of Your thoughts! Renew my mind, Lord Jesus, that I may be able to discover Your good, pleasing, and perfect will.*

71: WHEN YOU WANT REVENGE

Do not avenge yourselves, beloved, but leave room for God's wrath. For it is written: "Vengeance is Mine; I will repay, says the Lord." —Romans 12:19

When someone has hurt you so deeply that it takes months or even years to pick up the pieces, revenge can seem especially attractive. In those times of deep hurt, your flesh may say that revenge will bring justice, closure, and even healing to your heart, that inflicting pain on the one who hurt you will make your own pain disappear. But the Lord tells us not to avenge ourselves. Though justice will be served, it's not our job to serve it.

If your heart pushes back against that command, you're not alone. Revenge is a common human response to deep and lasting wounds. But if we rely on our hearts, we will be consumed by anger, and if we rely on our wisdom, we will enact justice on our own. When we desire revenge, the only answer is to rely on the Holy Spirit—to overcome the evil in the world and the evil in our own hearts.

In Romans 12:21, the apostle Paul writes, *"Do not be overcome by evil, but overcome evil with good."* When we take revenge, instead of getting closure, we continue the cycle of evil. Instead of overcoming evil, evil has overcome us. When we resist the desire for revenge with the help of the Holy Spirit, we break the cycle of evil. When we refuse to avenge ourselves, we're not minimizing the offense. We're not pretending there was no fallout. We're not even saying we don't want justice. We're simply surrendering our hurt and anger to the Lord, who has far more wisdom than we do to determine how justice should be served. It is only *then* that the process of closure and healing can begin.

If you are battling the desire for revenge, to repay evil for evil, ask the Holy Spirit to help you. Closure and healing will not come from a theatrical confrontation or from seeing the other person hurt in the way they hurt you. Peace will only come to your heart by unclenching your hands on this situation and surrendering it to the Lord, the only One who is perfectly just, perfectly wise, and perfectly loving.

Pray: *Lord God, my heart tells me that revenge will bring me closure and healing, but Your Word tells me not to avenge myself. Holy Spirit, empower me to not be overcome by evil, but to overcome evil with good.*

72: WHEN YOU WORK HARD IN THE LORD

Greet Tryphena and Tryphosa, women who have worked hard in the Lord. Greet my beloved Persis, who has worked very hard in the Lord.
—Romans 16:12

Tim Kizziar once said, "Our greatest fear as individuals and as a church should not be of failure but of succeeding at things in life that don't really matter."[7] In this brief commendation at the end of Paul's letter to the Romans, we read of three women who succeeded at what matters most: loving and serving the Lord with their whole hearts. We don't know much about Tryphena, Tryphosa, and Persis, but what we do know sets a beautiful example for us two thousand years later. They may not have had worldly accolades, but their work had eternal importance.

Paul's words bid us to reflect on how we approach our lives now. If we were to have a line written about us when we are gone, what would we want it to say? The world clamors for us to achieve position, amass wealth, or flaunt beauty, and many work hard to gain these things. This hard work is ultimately in vain—as Ecclesiastes 2:11 puts it, *"a pursuit of the wind."*

As followers of Jesus, though, our work has eternal value. We can endure hardships because we know it will be worth it. Paul doesn't detail exactly how

7. Tim Kizziar, quoted in Francis Chan, *Crazy Love: Overwhelmed by a Relentless God* (Colorado Springs: David C. Cook, 2013), 92.

these women *"worked hard in the Lord,"* and for our sake, that is a good thing; it isn't so much about what you do, but the heart behind it. From speaking the gospel to showing patience in your workplace to serving faithfully at your church, everything done for the Lord is precious in His sight.

What have you been working hard for? Are you directing your efforts at fruitful things that will last? As you consider the example of your sisters Tryphena, Tryphosa, and Persis, ask the Lord how you can follow in their footsteps with the talents and energy He has given you. Set your heart on succeeding in life at the things that truly matter and on the God who loves you, has called you, and has prepared good works for you to accomplish.

Pray: *Father, thank You for remembering Your daughters Tryphena, Tryphosa, and Persis in Your Word. I desire to be a woman like them, who works hard in You, putting my energy and talents toward work that will last.*

73: WHEN YOU FEEL UNKNOWN

For now we see only a reflection as in a mirror; then we shall see face to face. Now I know in part; then I shall know fully, even as I am fully known.
—1 Corinthians 13:12 (NIV)

In *The Meaning of Marriage*, Tim Keller writes, "To be loved but not known is comforting but superficial. To be known and not loved is our greatest fear. But to be fully known and truly loved is, well, a lot like being loved by God."[8] At the core of each human's heart is the desire to be deeply known and fully loved, but our temptation is to flip the script and chase the simile, the *like* more than the love Himself.

Although it's natural to long for a human to pursue our heart, study our story, and delight in us, putting our hopes in being sought by another person always ends in disappointment. Even those who try their best still can't come close to the way that the Lord knows you. In human relationships, something is always lost in the translation of your

---

8. Tim Keller, *The Meaning of Marriage: Facing the Complexities of Commitment with the Wisdom of God* (New York: Penguin Group, 2011), 101.

heart. The impossibility of full human understanding is actually a blessing in disguise, bidding you to shift your gaze from the finite creation to the infinite Creator, who *can* satisfy your heart's desire to be known and loved. No human can fully step into your experience, but if you are a believer, the Holy Spirit lives in you and inhabits your pain, joy, and the hidden things of your heart. The Lord is beyond language—nothing is lost in translation with Him. He doesn't need an interpreter for your heart because He created it.

First Corinthians 13:12 says, "*Now we see but a dim reflection as in a mirror.*" Right now, it's impossible to comprehend just how intimately God knows us and how deeply He loves us. We can see the shape of God's promises, but the details are blurred. One day, however, we will no longer have to look into a dull mirror. When we see Him face to face, we will understand that He has always been the answer to our longing to be loved and known.

Pray: *Father, You both know me fully and love me fully. Open my eyes to the depth of Your love and understanding that I may draw near to You, the only One who can wholly fulfill my deep desire to be known.*

74: WHEN YOU FEEL UNQUALIFIED

For God, who said, "Let light shine out of darkness," made His light shine in our hearts to give us the light of the knowledge of the glory of God in the face of Jesus Christ. Now we have this treasure in jars of clay to show that this surpassingly great power is from God and not from us.
—2 Corinthians 4:6–7

Have you ever feared that your weakness will tarnish your witness? Perhaps you struggle with anxiety and you're afraid others will think, "Some good her God is doing her—she's no different than us." Maybe you have a chronic health struggle, and you wonder if people will doubt God's power because you haven't been healed. Or you're a new believer just getting to know the Bible and you cringe when you imagine someone asking you a theological question. Any of these scenarios could tempt you to feel unqualified as an ambassador of Christ. But it is in our weakness that God works, shining His light through everyday people who are committed to Him.

The apostle Paul compares us to jars of clay that hold the light of God's glory out to the world. A jar of clay isn't that impressive in and of itself, and it isn't meant to be. What's important is what's *inside* the jar. As Christians, we have the most beautiful treasure inside that jar. Paul says all of this as one who feels his own weakness to the bone. He goes on to say, *"We are hard pressed on all sides, but not crushed; perplexed, but not in despair; persecuted, but not forsaken; struck down, but not destroyed"* (2 Corinthians 4:8–9). Paul was just as much a brittle jar of clay as we are, but his weakness had no bearing on what God did through him—powerfully shining His light across Europe and the Middle East in the first century and still shining through the very words you're reading today.

You may not feel qualified, but the only qualification you need, you already have. If you're a follower of Jesus, He will shine His light through you, period. Your strength has nothing to do with it. And when others see the light, your weakness is all the more proof that the power is from Him.

Pray: *Lord, I have feared that my weakness will dim Your light. Thank You for working powerfully in and through my weakness. I commit this jar of clay to You, trusting that You will shine Your light to the world around me.*

75: WHEN LIFE DISAPPOINTS US

For our light and momentary affliction is producing for us an eternal weight of glory that is far beyond comparison. So we fix our eyes not on what is seen, but on what is unseen. For what is seen is temporary, but what is unseen is eternal. —2 Corinthians 4:17–18

Disappointment can feel devastating. It's not just a feeling of sadness, but the destruction of something very real—your dearest dreams. Maybe another year has passed and you're still single when you long to be married. Maybe you desperately want to have to a baby, but year after year, the tests are negative. Perhaps you're battling a sudden health issue that has upended your life. Life has not turned out like you expected, and you feel hopeless as you survey the rubble of your dreams.

If this life is all we get, then each of these disappointments *is* a devastation. There is a quick shot at happiness and then … nothing. But if there is more to life than what we experience on this earth, disappointment doesn't have the last word. This is why every follower of Christ, no matter how disappointed, can say with confidence, "My best days are yet to come."

In John 16:33 (NIV), Jesus tells His disciples, *"In this world you will have trouble. But take heart! I have overcome the world."* Jesus knew that life on earth would disappoint, especially if we were to follow Him. He also knew that one day, regardless of what we have faced on earth, His presence would fulfill the longings that no human relationship ever could. Even if we were to receive all our earthly desires right now, we would still be unsatisfied until we see Jesus face to face.

If life's constant disappointments are tempting you to despair, remember that you are destined for an eternal joy beyond what you can imagine. Your affliction may not seem light and momentary, but in comparison to your eternal future, this is just a quick second of pain. One day, you will look back on this life with clear eyes and unending awe at how Jesus has eternally overcome the sadness, pain, and darkness you faced on earth.

Pray: *Father, my life is not what I've expected, and I'm disappointed about the dreams that haven't come true. Give me power to understand how light and momentary these struggles are and how You are kind and good through them all.*

76: WHEN YOU FEAR AGING

Now we know that if the earthly tent we live in is dismantled, we have a building from God, an eternal house in heaven, not built by human hands.
—2 Corinthians 5:1

It wasn't supposed to be this way. Our skin wasn't supposed to wrinkle and our hair to whiten, our bones to become brittle and our strength to fail. Aging comes with a unique angst—its presence is a long, drawn-out reminder that sin and death entered the world and are still enjoying their exploits. God did not design us to die, yet the lines on our faces and the weakening of our bodies tell us that nevertheless, we will. For the Christian, though, death is not something to be feared because it doesn't mark the end of our lives, but the beginning of the very best part—infinite, joyful life in the presence of Jesus. Aging is a reality, but aging does not have the last word.

The apostle Paul speaks of our bodies as tents—temporary homes compared to the buildings that God is preparing for us in in heaven. Without the hope of eternity, aging is certainly something to lament because regardless of how many Botox injections we get or supplements we take, our bodies—these earthly tents—are slowly but surely wearing out. Consider this, however: a camper on a short trip whose tent is dirtied and ripped by the elements doesn't despair but simply anticipates his return home all the more. The grime, cold, and rain are temporary; soon he'll be sleeping in his own bed, warm and clean. For those with the hope of eternity, aging isn't something to dread but a signpost toward heaven that makes us look forward to our homecoming even more.

When you fear aging, remember the future—this life is not all there is. This old, uncomfortable tent is temporary, and God promises to "*transform our lowly bodies to be like His glorious body*" (Philippians 3:21). We can have confidence in this because God has "*given us the Spirit as a pledge of what is to come*" (2 Corinthians 5:5), an eternity unmarred by sin, aging, or death.

Pray: *Father, when I fear aging, replace my earthly perspective with an eternal one. When I see the effects of aging, may I not despair, but praise You, as I consider that each day I get older brings me closer to eternity with You.*

77: WHEN YOU HEAR LIES ABOUT GOD

We tear down arguments and every presumption set up against the knowledge of God; and we take captive every thought to make it obedient to Christ. —2 Corinthians 10:5

The enemy has been lying to women about God since the very beginning. Eve heard the world's first lie from the serpent, whom God had created with a striking glory that pointed right back to His goodness. Yet the enemy tried to convince Eve that this goodness was all a lie.

God had told Eve and Adam that they could not eat of the tree in the center of the garden of Eden, but the serpent told Eve that God had been lying to them. "*You will not surely die,*" the serpent told her. "*For God knows that in the day you eat of it, your eyes will be opened and you will be like God, knowing good and evil*" (Genesis 3:4–5). The enemy's lie was as enticing as the fruit itself, and Eve let the lie captivate her with its promise of something better than what God had already given. Presuming that the enemy was telling the truth, she ate the fruit, allowing sin to enter and ravage the world.

Millennia after Eve's choice, Paul warns that our flesh is just as susceptible to the lies of the enemy. We need to go on the offensive, tearing down arguments that lie about God and prevent us from knowing Him as He truly is. Like Eve, our flesh can find certain lies captivating. These lies come in different forms, but at their root, they are the same as in the garden: God isn't as good as He claims to be.

How do you go on the offensive, taking the lie captive instead of being captivated yourself? God's Word is the most powerful weapon at your disposal. Scripture is not a mere collection of stories, proverbs, and history. It is the living, breathing expression of the truth. As you read of God's faithfulness to His people, His love in sending Jesus to die for you, and His power in resurrecting Him, the enemy's words are revealed for the lies they are. God is undeniably good, and the arguments against His goodness have no defense. With a mind empowered by God's Word, you can take any argument captive and lay it at Christ's feet, making it obedient to Him.

Pray: *Lord, You are good. Empower me to tear down the enemy's arguments against Your character and take those thoughts captive, not allowing them to ravage my mind and distort my knowledge of You. Holy Spirit, empower me to say no to the lies and to abide in You.*

78: WHEN YOU'RE PEOPLE-PLEASING

Am I now seeking the approval of men, or of God? Or am I striving to please men? If I were still trying to please men, I would not be a servant of Christ.
—Galatians 1:10

The apostle Paul tells us it's impossible to set your heart on both pleasing people and pleasing God. He practices what he preaches—when you read through his letters, you'll find many harsh rebukes that would be anything but pleasing to his readers. If Paul's goal was to maintain others' approval, he likely wouldn't have written so boldly. He had the courage to give these harsh but necessary words because his identity didn't rely on the opinions of others, but on the opinion of Christ.

Though you may not have to harshly rebuke entire churches, you still may be tempted to please people rather than God. If you're single, are you tempted to spend lots of time, money, and effort making yourself more attractive to men at the expense of caring for others? Do you avoid bringing up issues that may cause conflict even though the Holy Spirit is nudging you to speak? Or do you shy away from sharing the gospel because you're afraid of being thought of as strange or ignorant?

On the surface, these three examples seem to be about pleasing people, but they're actually about pleasing ourselves. The most loving things we do will sometimes be anything but pleasing to others, and when others aren't pleased, they just might reject us. It might not make your friend happy when you tell them they hurt you, but they won't have the opportunity to grow if they're unaware of the offense. You might seem strange or even offensive to a coworker when you share the gospel, but in doing so, you give them the opportunity to respond to Christ's love.

The fear of rejection may run deep, but as you lean into your identity in Christ—a solid identity unmoved by human disapproval—that fear takes a back seat. Replacing the fear of rejection with brave love for others springs from a commitment to being a servant of Christ, not a servant of others and not a servant of self. Pray that you would grow in your desire to be a servant of the Lord above all, and that He would give you the courage to love as He loves.

Pray: *Lord, I've been striving to please people more than You. Give me an undivided heart, that my love for You would embolden me to love others bravely, no matter how they respond.*

79: WHEN YOU'RE SEEKING GOD'S WILL

For we are God's workmanship, created in Christ Jesus to do good works, which God prepared in advance as our way of life. —Ephesians 2:10

Many Christians languish in fearful indecision because they don't understand the freedom God offers as we seek His will. Some view seeking God's will like choosing between two identical doors. One is God's will, the other isn't. If you choose the wrong one, your life will be ruined, and God will leave you to pick up the pieces. Morally neutral choices like moving away or staying put, taking this job or that one, become high-stakes tests that we think God has hidden the answers to. If this sounds like you, you may be missing out on the freedom you have in Christ. God *does* lead us to do specific things at times, but we miss the forest for the trees when we forget that our purpose lies not in the specific actions we take, but in the faith we take them with.

Ephesians 2:10 tells us that God has created us for good works. The positioning of this in the letter to the Ephesians is striking. Just a few sentences before this, Paul reminds the Ephesians that they have been saved by grace. It is *in* and *from* that grace that we act.

We live in a truly unique time in history. We have more choices about our career, location, entertainment, purchases, and relationships than those in past centuries could imagine, and this historical phenomenon has distorted our understanding of God's will. God's ultimate will is that we are sanctified, set apart for Him and becoming more like Christ with each passing day. (See 1 Thessalonians 4:3.) We are free to choose from a variety of options but when we make those choices, our hearts should be oriented toward becoming more like Jesus. In this process of sanctification, God gives us many opportunities to do good works.

Rather than fearing you will make a misstep in your big decisions, instead pray that God would reveal those good works He has for you *today*. You don't have to map out your entire life; you just need to be faithful in the here and now. The Lord will be faithful to lead you to those specific good works He has prepared for you, and as Paul says, to make them your "*way of life*."

Pray: *Father, show me the good works You have for me to do today. Help me to reflect Your love and walk in the Spirit in the mundane, unseen moments. Thank You for saving me by Your grace and giving me new life, that I may live for You.*

80: WHEN YOU WANT TO COMPLAIN

Do everything without complaining or arguing, so that you may be blameless and pure, children of God without fault in a crooked and perverse generation, in which you shine as lights in the world as you hold forth the word of life, in order that I may boast on the day of Christ that I did not run or labor in vain. —Philippians 2:14–16

Often the Scriptures that are the simplest to understand are the most difficult to put into practice. Do *everything* without complaining or arguing? Even when you're exhausted? Even when it's something no one seems to appreciate? Paul couldn't have meant that, right?

Complaining is woven into the fabric of our society. Venting negativity is seen as a healthy release of emotions, and complaining is a common way of bonding with others in less-than-ideal situations. To not complain seems … impossible. Still, the Lord calls us to it. In a world where complaining is commonplace, we will stand out as His followers in *"a crooked and perverse generation."*

This is not a call to toxic positivity. It's not putting a smile on your face when someone is struggling. It does not mean lament is forbidden. You can lament without complaining. Lament expresses pain and grief but surrenders it to the Lord, while complaining accuses the Lord of not being good enough. In fact, David Guzik comments that Paul's reference to complaining probably pointed back to Israel's grumbling over God's provision of manna in the desert.[9] Don't we do the same when we complain? Doesn't our complaining stem from a sense of entitlement, that God hasn't given us the lot in life we deserve?

The antidote to complaining is humble contentment. Israel could have approached the manna in the desert as miraculous provision from a loving God, but they viewed it as bland, boring, and unworthy of them. We will stand out to a discontented world when we praise God for His provision instead of complaining. The more you reflect on how He has provided, the more contented your heart will become. And as Jesus said, *"Out of the overflow of the heart, the mouth speaks"* (Matthew 12:34). With a contented heart, your lips will speak words of thanksgiving rather than complaining, giving a generation held captive by sin and perversion a window into the love, generosity, and provision of the One who longs for them to know Him too.

---

9. David Guzik, "Philippians 2 – Humble Living in Light of Jesus' Humble Example," Enduring Word Bible Commentary, enduringword.com/bible-commentary/philippians-2.

Pray: *Lord, may I fix my eyes on Your provision and goodness when I want to complain. Help my heart to overflow with contentment that others may see Your goodness and want to know You as well.*

81: WHEN YOU FEEL ANXIOUS

The Lord is near. Be anxious for nothing, but in everything, by prayer and petition, with thanksgiving, present your requests to God. And the peace of God, which surpasses all understanding, will guard your hearts and your minds in Christ Jesus. —Philippians 4:5–7

If anyone could understand anxiety, it would be the apostle Paul. For years on end, his life was filled with change, conflict, loneliness, and persecution. He wrote this very encouragement to the Philippian church from prison, knowing that each day might be his last. Even while facing imprisonment and the threat of death, Paul was comforted by a truth that we too can cling to when we feel anxious: *the Lord is near.* Meditating on the Lord's close proximity helps us to see things as they *are* rather than as we *feel*. Anxiety tells the lie that God is uninvolved in your life and that you have to figure things out on your own, but by fixing your mind on the Lord's nearness, you can rest in the reality that God is intimately involved in the details of your life.

Are you believing anxiety's lie that you need to solve all your issues by yourself? If anxiety is overwhelming you, let the truth that *the Lord is near* bring you comfort and peace. When your thoughts race and your mind dwells on worst-case scenarios, know that the God who created you masterfully, understands you intimately, and loves you fiercely knows exactly what you are facing and what you need. The same God who showed his nearness to the apostle Paul is the God who is near to you in your anxiety.

The beloved minister Oswald Chambers expresses this beautifully: "Fill your mind with the thought that God is there. And once your mind is truly filled with that thought, when you experience difficulties it will be as easy as breathing for you to remember, 'My heavenly Father knows all about this!'"[10] God not only knows the difficulties you face in the present, but He walks with you into your future, holding your hand and guiding your steps when you can't see the road ahead. Your heavenly Father is *always* near, and you are *never* alone.

Pray: *Heavenly Father, You are ever near, holding my hand as this wave of anxiety crashes against me. I give You my racing thoughts and anxious heart, trusting You for peace that transcends my understanding.*

82: WHEN YOUR THOUGHTS SPIRAL

Finally, brothers, whatever is true, whatever is honorable, whatever is right, whatever is pure, whatever is lovely, whatever is admirable—if anything is excellent or praiseworthy—think on these things. —Philippians 4:8

When your thoughts start to spiral, what's your first instinct? Many of us try to talk ourselves out of our anxious thoughts, thinking that if we analyze them from every angle, we'll be able to unearth some insight that will finally set us free from the thoughts that haunt us. This strategy may actually work against us in the battle of the mind.

In his book *Finding Quiet,* theologian J. P. Moreland explains that fighting toxic thoughts by analyzing why they aren't true actually reinforces them, keeping the neural pathways they travel well-oiled.[11]

Often our strategy is just that—to ruminate, determined to kill the negative thoughts—but fighting distorted thinking with the logic of the mind where such thinking resides doesn't make much sense. Instead, we need to "*dismiss the message,*" as Moreland says, by acknowledging that the thought is a lie and refocusing our attention on the truth.

Instead of punishing yourself for your anxious thoughts, submit them to God and redirect your attention to something good and true. This can often be something concrete and seemingly unspiritual but is

10. Oswald Chambers, "The Concept of Divine Control," *My Utmost for His Highest,* utmost.org/updated/the-concept-of-divine-control.
11. J. P. Moreland, *Finding Quiet: My Story of Overcoming Anxiety and the Practices that Brought Peace* (Grand Rapids, MI: Zondervan, 2019).

actually completely spiritual because it's a gift from God. It could be watching a funny show, calling a friend, doing a puzzle, or trying a new recipe—anything to engage your mind in something good.

Freedom from spiraling thoughts can seem impossible, but by resting from the fight in your mind and redirecting it to something good and true, you show trust that God will fight for you. No amount of analysis on your part will lead to freedom; instead, victory will only come when we rest our weary minds, submit our thoughts to Him and say, "Lord, only You can fight this battle."

Pray: *Lord, when my thoughts spiral, I tend to ruminate or try to make the thoughts go away. Please bring to my mind the things that are good, true, and praiseworthy and to trust You to renew my mind.*

83: WHEN YOU'RE DISCONTENT

I know how to live humbly, and I know how to abound. I am accustomed to any and every situation—to being filled and being hungry, to having plenty and having need. I can do all things through Christ who gives me strength.
—Philippians 4:12–13

If you've ever been camping, you know that it's nothing like being at home. Forget about a shower—if you're lucky, there's a nearby lake to wash in. The ground beneath your thin tent is likely uneven, and you wake up with aches and pains you've never experienced while sleeping in your own bed. But when you're camping, these inconveniences don't drive you to despair because you know your stay is temporary.

The apostle Paul went through things that would make the most optimistic person discontent, including "*beatings, imprisonments, and riots … labor, sleepless nights, and hunger*" (2 Corinthians 6:5). Yet in his letter to the Philippians, he expresses contentment. Paul knew he was just camping out, so he could be content with in his trials while he looked toward the heavenly home Jesus was preparing for him.

It's with this perspective that we can approach contentment. If this world is all there is, then we have reason to be discontent. The world is a dark place, and even our best days are tarnished by sin. As Paul says in 1 Corinthians 15:19, *"If our hope in Christ is for this life alone, we are to be pitied more than all men."* But our hope in Christ is for our future with Him. If we remember this, we will be strengthened to face the difficulties of a fallen world, knowing that this is only a temporary assignment.

When we're in financial need, we can remember our true riches in Christ while trusting that He'll provide for our earthly needs. When we're struggling with loneliness and broken relationships, we can look forward to the day when we will see Jesus face to face and all our relational desires will be met. When our health fails us, we can know that very soon, He will restore our bodies and heal all our sicknesses. Like Paul, we can be content in any circumstance not because of our own optimism or grit, but because of Jesus Christ, who strengthens us in the present with our future hope.

Pray: *Jesus, I need Your strength to be content right now. Please give me an eternal perspective, so I may remember that these trials are temporary, but my life with You is forever.*

84: WHEN A FELLOW CHRISTIAN HAS HURT YOU

Therefore, as the elect of God, holy and beloved, clothe yourselves with hearts of compassion, kindness, humility, gentleness, and patience. Bear with one another and forgive any complaint you may have against someone else. Forgive as the Lord forgave you. —Colossians 3:12–13

Have you ever found it harder to forgive a fellow Christian than someone who doesn't follow the Lord? When an unbeliever hurts us, the thought that they don't know any better can make us feel more gracious. They don't follow Jesus, so why would we expect them to follow His commands? But when another Christian speaks sharply to us, acts selfishly, or gossips carelessly, forgiveness can be harder to come by. "They should know better," we think.

Paul's words hint that the Christians in Colossae may have felt the same hesitation to forgive one another. Even though through Christ, we are righteous in God's eyes, while on earth, Christians still sin against one another. It was no different in the early church. The Christian response when we hurt others is what sets us apart from the world. As Paul exhorts the Colossians to forgive, he challenges any hesitation they have by reminding them of *who they are* and *what Christ has done*.

Paul reminds us that we are *"holy and beloved."* Our identity is no longer in our sinful nature, and we are no longer separated from God. When we remember that the person who hurt us is holy and beloved by God, we can better see them through the eyes of God's grace.

Paul also exhorts us to *"forgive as the Lord forgave you."* When we refuse to forgive, it often stems from pride, from believing we have the moral high ground over the person who hurt us. When we put their offenses beside God's great forgiveness of our sin, our hearts are humbled. When we remember that God has forgiven us for every sin against Him, forgiveness for others flows more freely.

We will inevitably hurt one another, but the Lord has shown us both how and why to forgive. And when we forgive one another, the church will stand out to the world, reflecting the lavish forgiveness of Christ.

Pray: *Father, I confess how hard it is to forgive believers who have hurt me. Help me to see others through the eyes of Your love and forgiveness, that I may forgive others as You have forgiven me.*

85: WHEN GOD IS REFINING YOUR FAITH

In this you greatly rejoice, though now for a little while you may have had to suffer grief in various trials so that the proven character of your faith—more precious than gold, which perishes even though refined by fire—may result in praise, glory, and honor at the revelation of Jesus Christ. —1 Peter 1:6–7

God never wastes your suffering. Peter doesn't just say this; he testifies to it with the story of his life. The genuineness of His faith was first tested when Jesus was arrested and three people asked Peter if he was one of Jesus's followers. Three times, he denied his Lord, but Jesus didn't give up on him. After Jesus restored him and sent him on a mission to shepherd the church, Peter underwent immense suffering that, according to tradition, culminated in being crucified upside down. God used these sufferings as refining fire for Peter, both strengthening his faith and bringing glory to God.

Peter's life shows us how the Lord wants to make our faith stronger, not weaker, through trials. In every trial, the Lord strips away that which is unimportant, showing worldly things for their fleeting nature and highlighting what is important—our eternal home with Him. When Peter says, *"In this you greatly rejoice,"* he's not speaking of the suffering itself, but of the hope we have for *"an inheritance that is imperishable, undefiled, and unfading, reserved in heaven"* (1 Peter 1:4).

If we didn't suffer at all, we would remain immature Christians with only a shallow gratefulness for our salvation, not understanding the depths of the darkness we have been saved from. We would go through our days skimming the surface of reality, not relying on the Savior who redeemed us or hoping in the future that awaits us. Suffering is not good for suffering's sake, but God uses suffering as a powerful tool to refine us, like fire refines gold. When the dross separates from the ore, solid gold is revealed, and we begin to understand just what a treasure our faith is.

Pray: *Father, I do not want to suffer, but I thank You that You use suffering to separate the dross from the ore, proving my faith genuine. Help me to suffer well and to stay faithful to You whatever comes, rejoicing in the imperishable inheritance waiting for me.*

86: WHEN YOU PREPARE YOUR MIND FOR ACTION

Therefore prepare your minds for action. Be sober-minded. Set your hope fully on the grace to be given you at the revelation of Jesus Christ. —1 Peter 1:13

When aspiring surgeons are attending medical school, they put in the painstaking work of memorizing the intricacies of human anatomy so that they can do good, not harm, during surgeries they will be performing in the future. There is purpose in the preparation. They are not learning just to obtain head knowledge, but to prepare their minds for action.

The goal of the Christian is much the same; our minds must be so thoroughly filled with the truth that acting on it is muscle memory. We have more knowledge available to us today than ever before. We have access to numerous translations of Scripture, can find hundreds of faith-based podcasts, and can obtain degrees in theology, biblical studies, Christian ministry, and the like if we desire. But all the head knowledge in the world doesn't necessarily translate into action.

We can be theologically astute while still having the muscle memory of the world, which acts on emotion and desire. When wronged, it returns hurt for hurt. When rejected, it people-pleases. When struck by tragedy, it despairs. When we catch ourselves responding in line with the world, the answer isn't necessarily to listen to another sermon or brush up on biblical Greek. It's much simpler than that.

We can prepare our minds for holy action by standing in awe of what Jesus has done for us daily. This doesn't require a theology degree, but it does require perseverance and humility. Though we are the Lord's, our own pride can tempt us to think we are *beyond* the gospel and that we need to move on to more complicated theological matters. But when the gospel loses its central place in our lives, our minds will not be prepared to act in line with it. It's a gift to have access to so much knowledge but we cannot let it distract us from the solid core of our faith.

When we cultivate a gospel-centered life, we cultivate the muscle memory that acts on truth and hope. When wronged, it forgives. When rejected, it rejoices that our Creator accepts us. And always, it sets our minds on our future hope, the grace to be revealed fully when we see Jesus face to face.

Pray: *Father, help me to prepare my mind for action by recounting the beauty and wonder of Your salvation! Develop in me the muscle memory that acts in truth and hope.*

87: WHEN YOU'RE FOCUSING ON YOUR APPEARANCE

Your beauty should not come from outward adornment, such as braided hair or gold jewelry or fine clothes, but from the inner disposition of your heart, the unfading beauty of a gentle and quiet spirit, which is precious in God's sight. —1 Peter 3:3–4

If no one but the Lord sees you, are you okay with that?

There's nothing inherently wrong with outward adornment. A flattering dress or a new hairstyle can be fun, feminine ways to express yourself. But outward adornment can have a dark side, one deeply connected to our desire to loved. "If only I stood out more," our hearts say, "then they would notice me. If only I were more beautiful, then he would love me." No longer is applying mascara and blush a neutral morning ritual, but a desperate attempt to be seen and loved.

Many of us have been locked in this prison of striving for years, but God offers us an escape through His definition of feminine beauty. In God's eyes, a beautiful woman isn't the one who stands out in a crowd for her striking looks or flawless figure. To Him, a woman is beautiful because of a gentle and quiet spirit, one that does not fear being unseen by the world, because in the Lord, she has all she needs.

Having a gentle, quiet spirit doesn't mean you need to change your personality—God has created some of us as extroverted and bold. It simply means that whatever your personality, your heart rests in the Lord and is free from the striving that holds so many women captive. The woman with a gentle and quiet spirit doesn't try to manipulate others' opinions of her through how she dresses or appears.

If you love style and getting glammed up, this isn't a call to throw away your red lipstick. It is a call to a freedom that few have experienced. When your greatest desire is not for others to notice you but to embody the Lord's definition of beauty, you are one of the freest women on earth, not dominated by the opinions of others or held captive by fear of being unloved. Embrace your freedom as a daughter of God and pursue the unfading beauty that is precious in His sight.

Pray: *Lord, I want to be free of my captivity to what others think of me. Help me to cultivate a gentle and quiet spirit that doesn't clamor for human approval, but rests in You.*

88: WHEN YOU'RE WORRIED

Cast all your anxiety on Him, because He cares for you. —1 Peter 5:7

When you pray, could you be praying to yourself?

If prayer typically leads to more anxiety than peace, this might be the case. When we lean on our own understanding during prayer, when we ruminate on the problem, trying to scan it for a solution that we can enact in our own strength, we're not casting our cares on God, but on ourselves. Sometimes, we do have a specific solution, but we don't have the power to enact it. At those times, we spend anxious hours trying to convince God to do our will, as though we're a lawyer making a case before an indifferent judge. Tim Keller says it well; often when we pray, he says, we are essentially "worrying in God's direction."[12] Why do we do this? Why do we become more anxious and more distant from God the more we pray? For many of us, the answer is we don't think He really cares for us.

The apostle Peter tells us that this isn't true. The Lord *does* care for us, and this knowledge changes everything. God is not distant, nor do we

12. Tim Keller, *Prayer: Experiencing Awe and Intimacy with God* (New York: Penguin, 2014), 85.

have to fight for His attention. What if we truly believed God's Word on the matter? If we truly believed He cared, we would end our prayers in a state of peace, not anxiety. If we truly believed He cared, we wouldn't strive to make an airtight case, but we would trust that He already had the solution and it's better than ours. If we truly believed He cared, we would cast our cares on Him, trusting that He has far stronger shoulders than ours and can carry them better and lead us along the very best paths for our lives.

The next time you pray, don't pray to yourself. Instead, dare to release your cares to the One whose words created the world, who led His people out of Egypt, who sacrificed Himself on the cross for your sake, and who knows the number of hairs on your head. He is faithful, He is good, and He cares for you.

Pray: *Lord, when I pray, may I not clutch my anxiety close, but cast my cares on You. When my heart is filled with the anxiety, remind me that You are with me and that You care deeply. You tell a greater story than I ever could, and I can trust You.*

89: WHEN YOU WANT TO LEAVE A LEGACY OF FAITH

I am reminded of your sincere faith, which first dwelt in your grandmother Lois and your mother Eunice, and I am convinced is in you as well.
—2 Timothy 1:5

No matter where you live, what work you do, or whether you have your own children, you can leave a legacy of faith. We don't know much about Lois and Eunice, but we do know that the way they steadily followed Jesus profoundly affected the young man God had entrusted to them. Their faithfulness inspired faith in Timothy, who himself became a faithful leader in the early church. Lois and Eunice teach us two things as we consider how we can leave a legacy of faith.

First, Lois and Eunice's faith was *sincere*. Their faith was not a mask they put on when they left the house. It was who they were, through and through, and as a family member, Timothy had a front row seat to the genuineness of their faith. Timothy saw the integrity of their lives and knew they were the real deal.

Lois and Eunice also left a legacy through their dedication to sharing God's Word. The apostle Paul wrote his two letters to Timothy around thirty years after the death and resurrection of Jesus, which makes it likely that Lois and Eunice were among the first Christians. These faithful women taught Timothy the Scriptures from a young age (see 2 Timothy 3:14–15), and these Scriptures took root in Timothy's life and led him to a knowledge of the truth.

As you seek the Lord with a sincere heart, look for the opportunities He gives you to pour into others. Share your life with them and share the Word of God. Leaving a legacy is often quiet, steady work, the long germination of the seed beneath the soil. You may not yet see the fruit, but your sowing is not in vain. When Lois and Eunice were living their everyday lives, bringing up Timothy in the Lord, they had no idea that countless people would be reading of the work God did through him, through his sincere faith *that first lived in them*. You too can trust that God will use your steady faithfulness to leave a legacy of faith for the next generation.

Pray: *Lord, I want to leave a legacy of faith. Create in me a sincere heart and give me opportunities to share Your Word with others.*

90: WHEN YOU'RE TRYING TO EARN LOVE

But when the kindness of God our Savior and His love for mankind appeared, He saved us, not by the righteous deeds we had done, but according to His mercy, through the washing of new birth and renewal by the Holy Spirit. —Titus 3:4–5

Unrequited love is a reality too many women are familiar with. Many who have experienced its sting find voice for their sorrow in the story of Leah, Jacob's unloved wife. (See Genesis 29.) As she watched her sister and rival wife Rachel receive the love she desired, Leah thought that bringing a son into the world might earn Jacob's love. "Surely, he will love me now," she thought. After the birth of child after child, she hoped that this time, she would have finally done enough to earn Jacob's love. But she never did.

Many of us have followed in Leah's footsteps, doing everything we can to earn someone's affection, only to be met with indifference. If we view love as something to be earned, then this indifference seems a reason for despair—if our best wasn't good enough, do we have any chance at being loved? The gospel provides such a sharp contrast to this Leah-like thinking, one that transforms our definition of love from something earned to something freely given.

With Jesus, there is no striving on your part and no withholding of love on His. Titus 3:4–5 tells us that Christ's love has nothing to do with any righteous works you have done or could do. Whereas Leah pursued Jacob, hoping that her performance would earn her just a crumb of affection, Jesus pursues you! Jesus saved you because of His great love and kindness, which were not sparked by waving your arms, trying to get Him to notice you, but an eternal love and kindness that existed long before you were born. You can be secure in His love, a love that you didn't earn, because He loved you first. (See 1 John 4:19.)

If you've been trying to earn love, let this be your call to cease striving. The love your heart desires is not earned but freely given, and that desire is fully met in the love of your Savior.

Pray: *Jesus, thank You for pursuing me with Your love. With You, I do not have to strive and I do not have to earn—I can simply rest. Guide me into a deeper understanding of Your love and the knowledge that I need not strive to earn Your love, but simply to love You back.*

91: WHEN YOU'RE WEAK

For we do not have a high priest who is unable to sympathize with our weaknesses, but we have one who was tempted in every way that we are, yet was without sin. Let us then approach the throne of grace with confidence, so that we may receive mercy and find grace to help us in our time of need.
—Hebrews 4:15–16

When you're at your lowest, there's nothing more comforting than talking with someone who understands. When they not only care but have been there too, you don't feel so alone. This is the beauty of how God wrote the story of our salvation. God chose to save us through the Word made flesh, a Savior who not only saved us from our sins, but who truly understands our weaknesses, temptations, and pain.

Jesus understands the frustration you feel when working with different personalities; He led a group of disciples from diverse backgrounds. He knows what it is to be tempted to put earthly things above His Father; Satan tempted Him with power and prestige if only He would bow down to him. Jesus knows what it's like to be single; He never married, while most Jewish men around Him did. Jesus knows what it is to be in excruciating pain; in fact, the word *excruciating* comes from the agony of crucifixion. He knows what it is to grieve the death of a family member; His beloved cousin John the Baptist was brutally murdered. He knows the pain of betrayal; one of His own disciples turned on Him. He knows what it's like to have prayers answered differently than He wanted; He pleaded for the Father to take the cup of crucifixion from Him, yet He submitted to His Father's will. Whatever experience you've had, Jesus had too.

The next time you are struggling with weakness, remember that your Savior is not far off. He is near and He fully empathizes because He has been there too. You can run to Him for grace in your time of need. He will not turn you away. He will listen, He will comfort, and He will strengthen you with His grace.

Pray: *Lord Jesus, I praise You for willingly taking on flesh and living as a human although it brought You great struggle and pain. I am thankful that You understand the deepest places of my heart because You've experienced the full spectrum of human life.*

92: WHEN YOU FEEL UNNOTICED

For God is not unjust. He will not forget your work and the love you have shown for His name as you have ministered to the saints and continue to do so. —Hebrews 6:10

About 91 percent of Jesus's life was unseen and undocumented. We tend to focus on His three-year ministry—on the miracles, the parables, and of course, His death and resurrection. But we can't forget this: the thirty years before His ministry were paced by the rhythms of the mundane. His movements were not made holy by their visibility, but by the fact that it was Him living and working as a human just like us.

For most of us, our lives are much the same. We'll have moments of visibility, chances to do *big* things, but regardless of the work we do or the country we live in, probably at least 91 percent is spent in the mundane: hitting the snooze button for the third time before a day filled with spreadsheets, emails, meetings, grocery shopping, and getting ready to do it all over again.

It is easy to feel that the unseen parts of our life aren't worth much, and that the mundane tasks are worth far less than the big, visible things like speaking on a stage, writing a book, or traveling across the world to do missions. When you're tempted to feel that the unseen parts of your life don't matter, remember the untold life of Jesus in the routine rhythms of a carpenter, where He was obedient to His Father when no one was watching. Don't mistake the mundane for wasted time because a hidden heart submitted to God, waiting for direction from the Holy Spirit, greatly pleases the Lord.

Take heart that He will use you powerfully right where you are, in the daily rhythms of your job and family and community. Take heart that He sees the motives behind the actions, and that an unseen act done out of love for Him is precious in His sight. And take heart that your effectiveness in His kingdom is not measured by numbers and visibility, but by obedience and faith. Others may not see what you are doing, but He does, and He will not forget your day-in, day-out faithfulness to Him in the hidden places.

Pray: *Jesus, thank You for Your example of unseen faithfulness in the mundane. I commit the unseen parts of my life to You. Help me to be faithful and to believe that You won't forget even my smallest act of faithfulness.*

93: WHEN YOU'RE ASHAMED OF YOUR PAST

By faith the prostitute Rahab, because she welcomed the spies in peace, did not perish with those who were disobedient. —Hebrews 11:31

In two out of the three times Rahab is mentioned in the New Testament—in this verse and James 2:25—she's referred to as a prostitute, a life she ultimately left. Only Matthew 1:5, which lists Jesus's genealogy, does not do so. We don't often see people named by their sins in Scripture; we don't read "the murderer David" or "the persecutor Paul," so at first glance, it may seem Rahab is being dealt an unfair hand. On second glance though, you'll notice that her former profession is followed by words that commend her faith in the one true God, faith God counted as a righteousness that rendered her former life powerless to keep her from salvation.

Rahab's story paints an early picture of the gospel that tells us nothing is outside of God's forgiveness. When Israelite spies came to Jericho, she hid them because she feared the Lord, knowing that her city, no matter how fortified, was no match for Him. In faith, she asked for them to spare her family's life when they attacked, and the spies agreed. The day when they stormed the city, the men stayed true to their promise. Not only were Rahab and her family spared, but she married an Israelite and became the mother of Boaz, the great-grandfather of King David, the ancestor of Jesus Christ. The Lord honored Rahab's faith, grafting her into His family and giving her the honor of ushering in the long-awaited Messiah.

Whatever your past, let the account of Rahab point you to the forgiveness Jesus offers. Rahab *was* a prostitute, but she didn't remain one. If you're a follower of Jesus, your sins no longer define you. As the apostle Paul says, *"Do you not know that the wicked will not inherit the kingdom of God? ... **And that is what some of you were.** But you were washed, you were sanctified, you were justified, in the name of the Lord Jesus Christ and by the Spirit of our God"* (1 Corinthians 6:9, 11).

If you feel you're too far gone for God to forgive you, remember how He accepted Rahab with open arms. When the label of your sin comes back to haunt you, remember that it no longer has any power because Christ has grafted you into His family.

Pray: *Father, thank You for telling the story of Rahab in Your Word, for showing me how You do not hold our sins against us, but offer full forgiveness. In You, I do not need to be ashamed. My past sins do not define me. You do.*

94: WHEN LIFE IS CONSTANTLY CHANGING

Jesus Christ is the same yesterday and today and forever. —Hebrews 13:8

Deep inside many women's hearts is the desire for security, stability, a *constant*. But for many of us, the only constant is *constant* change. From changing jobs to moving, from watching your child toddle to watching them leave home, from the start of a promising relationship to its sudden end, life is continually shifting.

When things change, it's second nature for many of us to frantically search for a person who will never leave us or forsake us. We think that if we just had the security of that one relationship, then we would be okay. But even when we forge stable relationships, this frantic fear in our hearts never quite goes away, because deep down, we know that nothing on earth has the promise of permanence.

In this frantic search for a constant, we often find ourselves beaten, bloodied, and fearful when our desired constant fails us. Commentator Alexander Maclaren gives a poetic description of what happens when we tie our desire for a constant to anything other than God:

> We give perishable things supreme power over us, and so intertwine our being with theirs, that the blow which destroys them lets out our life-blood. And, therefore, we are ever disturbed by apprehensions and shaken by fears. We tie ourselves to these outward possessions, as Alpine travellers to their guides, and so, when they slip on the icy slopes, their fall is our death.[13]

For the Christian, the fall of earthly things does not have to be our death! Though our lives on earth may constantly be change, we *do* have the constant we long for, and His name is Jesus. Hebrews 13:8 tells us that Jesus has never changed and will never change. He is the love you long for. He knows the number of hairs on your head. He cares for you. He has forgiven you. He is *"the way and the truth and the life"* (John 14:6). He will never leave you nor forsake you.

Dear sister, the constant you long for has constantly loved you through the ebbs and flows of human relationships, through the moves and seasons and joys and heartbreaks. Cling to Him when life changes because He is steadfast.

Pray: *Jesus, I feel tossed to and fro right now by the constant change in my life. I long for security and stability. Please show me if I have been seeking security in the wrong places and help me to experience the security of Your constant, unchangeable love.*

---

13. Maclaren, *Expositions of Holy Scripture, Vol. 3*, 254.

95: WHEN YOU PRAY FOR OTHERS

Therefore confess your sins to each other and pray for each other so that you may be healed. The prayer of a righteous man has great power to prevail. Elijah was a man just like us. He prayed earnestly that it would not rain, and it did not rain on the land for three and a half years. Again he prayed, and the heavens gave rain, and the earth yielded its crops. —James 5:16–18

Have you ever promised to pray for someone and immediately forgot to do so? Many of us habitually say, "I'll pray for you" but don't follow through. Why do we forget? The truth is, we don't usually forget what we believe will make a difference. We don't forget to go to work; otherwise, we'd be out of a job. We don't forget to eat because the hunger pangs tell us we need nourishment. The logical conclusion is that if we forget to pray, we don't truly believe it'll make a difference. James tells us that we are wrong—our prayers are powerful.

Many neglect prayer because their experiences have deceived them into thinking God doesn't answer. Perhaps you've prayed for a friend's healing but their cancer has only gotten worse. Or you've asked God for years to bring a godly spouse to a precious friend, but there's still no man in sight. This may seem like evidence that God doesn't hear or care, but James says that God doesn't only hear a select few, but *all* those who are His. Elijah was a human just like us, and God acted when he prayed.

When we pray, though, we must keep one thing in mind—if God answers differently than we ask, it's because He can see things we can't. Tim Keller puts it beautifully: "God will either give us what we ask for in prayer or give us what we would have asked for if we knew everything he knows."[14] God's answers to our prayers are mysterious, but we can trust that He will answer what is best and in the best timing.

The next time you offer to pray for a friend, trust that there is power in your intercession. Just as God heard Elijah, He hears you and will respond with the best possible answer.

14. Keller, *Prayer: Experiencing Awe and Intimacy with God*, 228.

Pray: *Lord, I confess I haven't believed that there is power in prayer. Help my unbelief and help me to view intercession as a powerful privilege You give to Your children. May Your will be done in my life and in the lives of my friends.*

96: WHEN YOU HAVE SINNED

If we confess our sins, He is faithful and just to forgive us our sins and to cleanse us from all unrighteousness. —1 John 1:9

This is a promise to every follower of Jesus Christ. There is no *maybe*, no condition; there is only forgiveness.

When we sin, we sometimes feel we are the exception, that we've fallen too far or sinned too much to ask for forgiveness yet again. How the enemy would love for us to believe this lie! When we confess our sins, He is *faithful*. What He *says* is what He *does*, and what He said with His sacrifice on the cross was that our sins were paid for, once and for all.

When we confess our sins, He is *just*. This is where our hearts fight against the truth. Deep down, we know that justice requires sacrifice for our sins. We know that without Christ, justice would mean that we would pay for our own sins. In our appeal to justice, we often forget that now, because of what Christ has done, He has made our forgiveness just! Although we deserve to pay for our sins, He has already done it. Justice has been served.

When we confess our sins, He *cleanses us from all unrighteousness*. We feel dirty after we sin. Driven by the impulse to cleanse ourselves, we often punish ourselves or try to hide our sins under good works. Again, the gospel tells us this is all wrong. We cannot clean ourselves up. It's like taking a shower while washing with a cloth covered in grime. We will only succeed in making ourselves dirtier. Jesus is the only one who can cleanse us, and He does so willingly and joyfully, His righteousness making it as though we'd never sinned.

When you have sinned, confess it to the Lord and have confidence in the words of the apostle John. Your Savior is faithful and just, and He washes you from the uncleanliness of your sins. Come boldly before Him, confess, and then press on as you follow in His steps.

Pray: *Father, I praise You for making a way for my forgiveness. When I feel I have fallen too far or too many times, remind me that You are faithful. You've said You will forgive and You will, and You are just—through Jesus's sacrifice, my debt has been paid.*

97: WHEN YOU NEED ASSURANCE OF SALVATION

If anyone confesses that Jesus is the Son of God, God abides in him, and he in God. And we have come to know and believe the love that God has for us. God is love; whoever abides in love abides in God, and God in him.
—1 John 4:15–16

William Cowper wrote many hymns we still treasure today, including the beloved song "There Is a Fountain Filled with Blood." One thing many people may not know is that Cowper battled severe mental illness. In his lowest moments, he questioned his salvation, believing that he was beyond grace. In Cowper's beautiful words, we see a man whose heart overflowed with love for Christ. But with a broken mind, he still doubted.

Like Cowper, many of us are haunted by the thought that *we might not really be saved*. The enemy's snakish lies that lead us to doubt our salvation are the very lies the gospel addresses. Cowper wrestled with the lie that his sin outweighed God's grace. It is true that Christlike love for others is evidence of our salvation, as we read throughout 1 John, but we will not be perfect in this life. We have been freed from the curse of sin *and* we still battle our sinful nature. But when we do sin, we do not have to fear losing our salvation. After all, we are saved not because of our goodness, but *His*.

The apostle John offers comfort for those times when our hearts doubt our salvation: "*Even if our hearts condemn us, God is greater than our hearts, and He knows all things"* (1 John 3:20). When our mind doubts and we feel beyond grace, God's mind is clear and unchanging—He knows all things, He know those who are His, and none of that changes, no matter how we feel.

If you have confessed that Jesus is the Son of God, He has begun a work in you that He will finish. (See Philippians 1:6.) When you doubt, remember what William Cowper preached to his own heart in his treasured hymn:

> There is a fountain filled with blood
> Drawn from Immanuel's veins;
> And sinners, plunged beneath that flood,
> Lose all their guilty stains.[15]

Pray: *Lord Jesus, I praise You for my salvation! I have confessed with my mouth that You are the Son of God, and I trust that You have cleansed me from my sins. You will finish what You started in me. I am thankful that when my heart condemns me, You are greater than my heart, and You know all things.*

98: WHEN YOU ARE WEEPING

"'He will wipe away every tear from their eyes,' and there will be no more death or mourning or crying or pain, for the former things have passed away." And the One seated on the throne said, "Behold, I make all things new." Then He said, "Write this down, for these words are faithful and true."
—Revelation 21:4–5

This world is a place of weeping. Each tear of disappointment, each wail of grief—all have the underlying cry that *things are not supposed to be this way*. You may even be weeping at this moment, and you wonder if your pain will ever end. Regardless of the depth of your pain or how long your suffering has been, you have a "*faithful and true*" promise from the God

15. William Cowper, "There Is a Fountain Filled with Blood," 1771.

who never lies: One day, death itself will pass away, and He will wipe every tear from your eyes.

If you're weeping in grief, one day, grieving will be no more, for death will be no more.

If you're weeping out of loneliness, one day, you'll be in the Lord's presence, and loneliness will be a thing of the past.

If you're weeping over unfulfilled desires, one day, there will be no disappointment.

Revelation, this final book in Scripture, speaks of the happy ending to the tragedy that began to unfold in Genesis, when sin and grief and weeping entered the world. All of Scripture is a story of God's redemption, and it culminates in the Lord making everything new.

Do you know the Lord who will make all things new? Who will wipe every tear from the eyes of His people? His name is Jesus Christ, and He calls you to Him right now, to proclaim Him as Lord, to cling to His promises in a dark world, and to wait for His return when, as Tim Keller says, "Everything sad is going to come untrue."[16]

Trust in Him while you weep because your weeping will be like the weeping of Mary Magdalene at the tomb. She thought she was mourning the death of her Lord, but Jesus stood in front of her, alive and victorious. Very soon, your faith will become sight, and your tears will vanish when you see His face, His kindness, and His glory.

Pray: *Jesus, my heart is grieved, and my weeping seems unending. You see every tear, and You have made a plan to banish death and make all things new. In my times of deepest grief, help me to remember that future and trust in You, for Your words are faithful and true.*

16. Tim Keller, *The Reason for God: Belief in an Age of Skepticism* (London: Penguin Random House, 2008), 33.

99: WHEN YOU'RE LOOKING FORWARD TO JESUS'S RETURN

He who testifies to these things says, "Yes, I am coming soon." Amen. Come, Lord Jesus! —Revelation 22:20

Jesus is coming soon.

You may be skeptical of these words at first glance. *Soon* doesn't seem to be the right word to describe the wait for Jesus's second coming. After all, the apostle John wrote down these words of Jesus nearly two thousand years ago, and we are still waiting for our Lord's return. Throughout two millennia, generation after generation of believers have read the words of Revelation and prayed that He might return during their lifetimes.

Soon for the Lord is not the same as soon for us. The apostle Peter tells us that any perceived delay is based on God's love and kindness, writing, *"Beloved, do not let this one thing escape your notice: With the Lord a day is like a thousand years, and a thousand years are like a day. The Lord is not slow in keeping His promise as some understand slowness, but is patient with you, not wanting anyone to perish but everyone to come to repentance"* (2 Peter 3:8–9).

Jesus is coming soon, but He hasn't come yet because He is waiting for more people to repent. He has invited us to play a part in this long story of redemption, and our anticipation of His return will help us to focus our lives not on ourselves, but on seeing others join His kingdom.

How would you live if you expected Jesus to return tomorrow? How would it reframe your unfulfilled desires, your trials, and your suffering? Who would you tell of Jesus's love, sacrifice, resurrection, and redemption? Though we don't know if Jesus will return in our lifetimes, we gain something beautiful when we remind ourselves that *it just might be today*: unblurred eyes and a clear perspective on life, death, and eternity. Daughter of God, live in light of your Savior's return. Act when the Holy Spirit moves you, even when you're scared. Lament your suffering but look forward to the day He will take it all away. And along with the apostle John, pray the words that countless Christians have repeated through the centuries, "Come, Lord Jesus!"

Pray: *Jesus, You are coming soon! Help me to live my life in light of Your return, growing in holiness, boldness, and love. I joyfully await seeing You face to face.*

ABOUT THE AUTHOR

Hope Johnson is a writer and editor who makes her home in Upstate New York. She is the host of *The Hope Unyielding Podcast,* where people from all walks of life share stories of God's faithfulness in dark and difficult times.

An avid traveler and language lover, Hope studied, taught, and volunteered in Russia and Belarus nine times between 2003–2019 and spent several years teaching English to international college students. She has a B.A. in Linguistics from Gordon College and a master's in Teaching English to Speakers of Other Languages (TESOL) from Biola University.

When she isn't writing, she enjoys adventuring to new places, reading Russian literature, and having deep conversations with friends.

Connect with Hope at hopeunyielding.com.